Rulers of the Land

From the Atlantic to the Pacific, from the Gulf of Mexico to the Canadian Rockies, in the great forests of the East, the fertile lands of the South, the unbroken expanses of the Great Plains, the American Indian reigned. His tribes shared a common ancestry but developed in sharply different ways—some farmers, some hunters, some excelling in war, some in the arts of peace, and all evolving toward their individual destinies. Then the white men came,—and all began to change...

American Epic is the story of what was lost, what was gained, and what must now be done.

"THIS BOOK SETS THE RECORD STRAIGHT ON THE HISTORY OF THE AMERICAN INDIAN."

—*Beaumont Journal*

ABOUT THE AUTHORS: ALICE MARRIOTT and CAROL K. RACHLIN are well-known anthropologists who have devoted many years of study to the American Indian, past and present. Miss Marriott served with the Indian Arts and Crafts Board of the Department of the Interior, and her books include *Greener Fields, Black Stone Knife, Sequoyah, The Ten Grandmothers*, an ethnological study of the Kiowas, and *Indians on Horseback*. Miss Rachlin has served as state archeologist for the New Jersey State Museum, research associate for the Indiana Historical Society, and consultant for the Museum of the Five Civilized Tribes in Oklahoma. Alice Marriott and Carol K. Rachlin are co-authors of *Peyote* and *American Indian Mythology*, also available in MENTOR editions.

American Epic

THE STORY OF THE AMERICAN INDIAN

by

Alice Marriott and Carol K. Rachlin

A MENTOR BOOK
NEW AMERICAN LIBRARY
TIMES MIRROR
NEW YORK AND SCARBOROUGH, ONTARIO

Library of Congress Catalog Card Number: 69-11463

This is an authorized reprint of a hardcover edition published by G. P. Putnam's Sons. The hardcover edition was published simultaneously in the Dominion of Canada by Longmans Canada Limited, Toronto.

MENTOR TRADEMARK REG. U.S. PAT. OFF. AND FOREIGN COUNTRIES
REGISTERED TRADEMARK—MARCA REGISTRADA
HECHO EN CHICAGO, U.S.A.

SIGNET, SIGNET CLASSICS, MENTOR, PLUME AND MERIDIAN BOOKS
are published by The New American Library, Inc.,
1301 Avenue of the Americas, New York, New York 10019,
in Canada by The New American Library of Canada Limited,
81 Mack Avenue, Scarborough, 704, Ontario

FIRST MENTOR PRINTING, OCTOBER, 1970

3 4 5 6 7 8 9 10 11

PRINTED IN THE UNITED STATES OF AMERICA

To

Our nieces and nephews—by blood and by adoption

Contents

Foreword

Very many books have been written about North American Indians and their cultures. Few such books have dealt specifically with the effects of European and Euro-American contacts on interrelations among the cultures of the New World.

It is our hope that in the following pages we can suggest, and perhaps develop, some of these complicated interplays. What would have been the effect on our nation's history if the Spaniards, instead of the French, had colonized the St. Lawrence River valley? What would have happened if North American Indian immigrants to Mexico had not returned northward and reoccupied the Mississippi drainage in the eleventh and twelfth centuries? If Europeans had stayed at home and minded their own business—had they been economically and socially able to do so—in the fifteenth and sixteenth centuries, would there have been a power struggle between Iroquoians and Athabascans in the heart of the continent? On and on the questions go, unrolling before us a scroll of possibilities.

It is not the intent of this book even to try to answer these provocations. Its purpose is simpler: to show what, within the scope of recorded history, actually did happen and interhappen. In some cases the writers have drawn not only on published or archival resources but on their own independent fieldwork: on what Indian informants said, from their and their ancestors' point of view, *did* happen. And the final collation has proved the differing records to be not far apart in the presentation of known facts.

This is not a book for a professional anthropologist. It is a book for a general reader who is interested in his own country, its background, the approaches of its founding fathers to various situations, and the hazards and struggles of a conquered people. The last phrase may lead to development of data that will suggest possible solutions to the problems of other conquering, conquered, and emerging nations.

For, tragedy or triumph—and it is both—the story of the North American Indians has its application elsewhere. Nowhere else in the world has a conquering nation set up a federal bureau to deal specifically with the problems of a people it has defeated. The Bureau of Indian Affairs of the Department of the Interior came into provisional existence (under the military) before the Constitution of the United States had been ratified, or any of its writers had thought of a Department of the Interior. The Bureau has continued to function to this day of writing, under one federal department or another. Good, bad, and often indifferent, the Bureau of Indian Affairs is *there*, unique and inseparable from the people whose lands it administers and whose destinies it indirectly controls. The two are as intertwined in Indian minds as firearms and bows and arrows.

ALICE MARRIOTT AND CAROL K. RACHLIN

Oklahoma City

January, 1969

American Epic

Part One

Migration

1

The First Wanderers

THE COASTLINE OF THE EASTERN OCEAN WAVERED AND stretched, curving southward. Its northern boundary was enclosed by a chain of mountains, joined to those of coastal Siberia on the west and to a southward-reaching cordillera on the east.

The same game animals were to be hunted at either end of the northern mountain chain and all along its uplifts. Woolly mammoths, giant sloths, bears, and great elk in particular dominated the landscape. The smaller game—weasels, hares, and rodents of many other kinds—were the same on each continent and lived on the same sort of tundra. The winds blew from north or south, and men steered against the sideward pressure of the winds, for the east-west chain was too narrow for its height, and north- or south-bound travel across its peaks was difficult.

There were the same fish in the waters on either side of the mountain chain. Whales, sculpins, salmon, and abalones and other kinds of shellfish could be taken. The animals of land and sea far outnumbered the men who hunted them or fished for them. If food was scarce in one place, it was possible, if not easy, to move on to another.

So the people journeyed eastward, and when the weather was cold, turned south. Before that turn, however, they had reached another ocean, even farther to the east, and before they reached the farthest eastern shore of the New World they had passed many great lakes and bays, for the easiest travel always followed the waterways.

The time was from ten to four thousand years ago. A continent is not occupied and reoccupied quickly, especially by peoples who have no transport but their own legs and those of their dogs, or rafts or canoes. Behind them the mountain chain connecting one mainland to another sank into the sea in one of those cataclysms that still rock the Pacific coasts, east and west. Only the dwellers along the coastline could have been conscious of the earthquake, or directly affected by it, for another two thousand years.

Other peoples probably came from the westward, too, drifting along the northeast set of the Japan current as the water took and held their fishing rafts. The seacoast where they landed was bare and desolate, the mountains rose to the skies behind them, but here again was food and a place to live. They had been coastal people in the islands they had once called their homes, and they remained coastal people on the new mainland where they had landed.

All these wanderers were human beings, as human beings are known today. Their posture was upright. The *foramen magnum* had taken the same position in relation to the spinal column that it has in modern man. Dentition was restricted to thirty-two teeth, divided between the upper and lower jaws. The lower incisors displayed one peculiarity: their inner surfaces were so deeply grooved as to resemble the lifting face of a shovel. The first wanderers were probably of short stature, as are most peoples who exist on a limited food supply. Their hair was black; their skins ranged in tone from bronze to copper, and the epicanthic folds at the outer corners of their eyes pulled the eyelids upward and outward, so that they appeared to slant above the flat, outward-flaring cheekbones. They were strong people, or families could not have endured and survived to leave descendants.

In the interglacial periods of the Pleistocene Age the climate was warm and damp. Vegetation flourished. Bamboos and other tropical grasses grew then where we know only microscopic Arctic blossoms now. In general, living was easy, although there seem to have been occasional drought periods that reduced the vegetation and cut down the supply of available game animals.

It was fortunate that living was comparatively easy, for mechanically and technologically the first wanderers in search of food had not perfected many weapons or implements. They knew how to make string, to be used for cords and snares. They had dogs, not only as beasts of burden but for hunting. And certainly the firstcomers knew of fire and of its use in cooking. They could dress skins, even though clothing was generally scanty or lacking.

There is much uncertainty among archaeologists as to the actual weapons and tools the wanderers brought with them. Some archaeologists speculate that the journey eastward began in central Siberia, at a time when stone flaking had not yet been developed. Tools of rubbed and ground stones were in use. In this case, weapons and tools must have been interchangeable. The same wooden-handled stone hammer could be used with equal ease to crack nuts, shellfish, or the skulls of cave bears and other enemies.

Certainly, later migrants brought the knowledge of, and considerable skill in, chipping stones. Woolly mammoths have been found entombed in the slowly thawing Arctic tundra with finely worked stone spearpoints or knives embedded in their flesh. Perhaps the spears were hurled with atlatls (spear throwers), which were the first projectile weapons known on the hemisphere. Bows and arrows came at a later date, with another wave of occupation.

Because there was no native population in the New World to be displaced or to become resistant, the first migrants could wander at will, year after century after millennium, until they occupied both hemispheres from Alaska to the tip of Cape Horn. Opposition to migrations did not begin until some of the first wanderers turned to retrace their steps and found other groups of people settled in the lands they had entered.

All these peoples had spoken languages. Much of the work of dating the diffusion of other culture traits has been done through language study. Root words and lip and tongue positions have been traced from place to place. Archaeolinguistics is a comparatively new field of research. Regrettably so, for had the analysis of languages been begun sooner many tongues would not have been blotted out. Research in linguistics could have been intensified and broadened.

To pause for a moment, it is interesting to note the many traits the earliest settlers of the Americas lacked. None of them knew of writing, either of sounds or of mathematical symbols. The wheel was nonexistent in their world. The last migrants may have known of sails, but no wanderer knew of wheels or of metalworking. Later, craftsmen discovered how to hammer and mold soft metals into ornaments. Metal tools and cutting edges were unknown in the Americas before European invasion. The plants of the New World differed widely from those of the

Old, and it is thought that American agriculture developed independently from that of Asia-Europa.

Dating, by any method, is always open to question. The most accurate method known to archaeologists at present is carbon-14 analysis. Materials which contain carbon (including all living matter, whether plant or animal) give off carbon particles at a known rate of release. By examination, it is possible to determine the carbon supply of a particular specimen. At present, the rate of accuracy of carbon-14 dating can be brought to plus/minus fifty years.

Paleontology naturally plays a large part in site dating. The strata in which specimens are found, and their association with living or extinct plant and animal forms, supply much comparative information. That is the reason archaeologists can speak knowingly of the Pleistocene Age, its periods, and life forms. Paleontologists told them.

Later, when human occupation of North America was firmly established, comparison of specimens, especially with relation to carbon-14 dates, could be employed for dating. The comparative method can be used to establish minimal and maximal dates and to determine the spread of culture traits from one part of the world to another.

Last, and most restricted geographically in its use, there is dendrochronology, or tree-ring dating. This method is based on the fact that certain types of trees, if they grow on the same watershed, develop annual growth rings whose patterns can be matched to one another. Dendrochronology is most useful in the southwestern states, where cycles of wetness and drought are most clearly reflected in the patterns of the growth rings.

Put them all together, and the various dating methods can reveal a great deal about when things happened, and even something about how they happened. It is the ever elusive *why* that remains still to be sought. The best answer to the *why* is: People were hungry.

The oldest remains of humanity in the Americas are scattered at least from Alaska to Florida, and are not human at all but stone. About 1925 a stone point was found near Folsom, New Mexico. It was embedded in the vertebra of a prehistoric—extinct—bison.

At first it was thought that the Folsom point, as it came to be called, was a local phenomenon of the High Plains country. As time went on, more and more of the laurel-leaf-shaped points, each with a deep groove running down the center of both faces, were found in spots where the wind had blown away the loose surface sand and exposed the stone beneath it. The points were not "primitive" in character; they were finely shaped, delicate, and made with skilled hands by expert workmen. There was nothing crude about the Folsom points. They were made of all kinds of stone: agate, chert, jasper, chalcedony—whatever the region afforded. They were made of anything and everything except flint, for there is no true flint to be found in the New World.

As time went on, Folsom, or "Folsomoid," points turned up all over the place. They were found buried with prehistoric—and extinct—mammoths in the frozen muck of the Alaskan tundra. Here the points were large, as if they had been used to tip heavy spears. Folsom points were also found in sites in the Mississippi Valley, where they were so small that they must have been tips for bird darts. They turned up in New York State and in Alabama. Only one generalization seems safe: Whoever made the points knew a good and useful weapon when he saw it, for the deep grooving on the faces was a quick conductor for the blood of a wounded animal.

Our information on preconquest life in North America comes from archaeologists who have excavated the sites where the early peoples lived. Prehistoric sites north of Mexico may be blowouts in the sand, like that of Folsom; they may be caves in bluffs or riverbanks, or they may be the remains of great cities.

Along the Atlantic coast there are many remains of fish-eating, and especially shellfish-eating, peoples. The archaeology of the eastern states is spotty. The earliest explorers were more interested in their own lives and towns than in those the Indians lived in before the Europeans came. Shell mounds were leveled to provide lime for fertilizer; Indian populations were wiped out.

After the time of wandering on foot, of gathering wild seeds and killing small game, there was a period of settlement, as the different groups of Indian wanderers found hospitable climates and ecologies and began to occupy their chosen terrains.

Some geographic areas were settled sparsely, while some others, in time, grew to considerable population density. Exact figures of early populations are lacking to us, of course, but probably the most accurate figure yet calculated on the basis of available food supply, known burials, and water sources is about 600,000 persons in North America, about the same figure as the American Indian population in the 1960 U.S. Census Report. Probably no more definite statement as to the aboriginal population of the Americas can be made.

Why the population of some areas grew and flourished more than that of others is equally hard to explain. There certainly never was an area less conducive to a population explosion than the desert of the North American southwest. But populations there grew to the explosion point, as they did elsewhere.

The sub-Arctic and sub-Antarctic areas remained as they had always been: places where a bare subsistence could be wrenched from the bitter climate to support a limited number of persons. In fact, so limiting were the natural factors of these areas that old persons or weak children often were not permitted to survive the bitter winters and to consume food that would support the productive members of their communities.

South, roughly from the coastal islands below Cape Hatteras to the Florida Keys, remnants of coastal peoples survive, together with their artifacts. As the inspection of sites turns westward and inland, there is an almost bewildering variety of cultures to be found, until coastal California is reached, with another very simple shell-midden people.

At the lowest level of identifiable occupation there is a homogenous culture, which existed wherever men did. This "Archaic" culture was sufficiently complex to show that its people had passed beyond simple wandering into more or less settled occupation of areas. It will be described more fully in later chapters.

We cannot separate what was happening in the Americas between 10,000 B.C. and the beginning of the period of exploration from what was happening in the rest of the world. This is particularly true if we think of what was going on in Europe, for if the first settlers of the Americas had come from the west, the developers and exploiters came from the east.

2

Across the Ocean

"The Atlantic River" was a reality long before 1969. Fishermen came and went across it, following schools of fish, landing to dry and pack down their catches, and returning to the markets of Stockholm, London, and Rotterdam to sell the food.

These northern European areas were on the fringes of European politics, art, religion, and literature until well into the sixteenth century. All the European world's attention was focused on the south, where in Italy and Spain particularly learning underwent a renaissance, then leaped ahead into the heresy of independent thinking. The center of the European's world was Rome, and after Rome, Seville. The northern countries, with their barbarous languages and old-fashioned folkways were the hinterlands. If the peoples who lived in the north regarded fish as a necessary food instead of a penance, let them eat fish. Even France was backward, compared with Italy and Spain.

The learning of the Renaissance cannot be decried, for its speculative attitude developed into what we know today as scientific thinking. While Columbus was standing eggs on end to prove that the world was round, the Swedes, the Dutch, the Irish, the English, and the Bretons were simply sailing back and forth across the North Atlantic, catching fish and cutting down trees, to bring timber and food home with them.

For the absorption of populations and the rise of the city-states, which characterized the end of the Middle Ages and the beginning of the Renaissance, were also beginning to deplete Europe's natural resources. There was need for wood for house building, ore smelting, and shipbuilding. As clothing grew more lavish and elegant, there was a need for furs and fibers. In fact, if the Americas had not existed, it would have been necessary for Europeans to invent them, or their equivalents.

The first European descriptions of American Indian cultures are incidentals, thrown in to fill out the record of natural resources and terrains. These people did not look like Europeans. They looked enough like Marco Polo's descriptions of Orientals, and the few Orientals who had made their way to Europe, to lead the first recording discoverer to call them "Indians" and the islands where they lived "the West Indies"; even to take a few captives back to Spain for exhibition at court.

The peoples of the Caribbean Islands lived in a warm climate, and their way of life was simple. There were fish in the sea, shellfish on the shore, and fruits, nuts, and berries growing inland. There was even some gold in the streams, which the simple people, not knowing its value, merely worked into ornaments by pounding it with stones or engraving it with sharp-pointed shells.

There was enough gold, at any rate, to awaken interest in all southern Europe. Spain claimed the West Indies and all lands adjacent, but the king of Portugal prevailed on the Pope, Alexander Borgia, to draw a "line of demarcation," which theoretically, at least, divided the New World between Portugal and Spain.

Word of the claims to the New World reached England and the ears of thrifty King Henry VII. Gold would be nice and valuable spices even nicer, but Henry was more concerned about his fishing grounds and timber resources than he was about niceties. He commissioned John Cabot and his son Sebastian, both Italians, to sail the North Atlantic and to claim as much land as they could. If, incidentally, they found the Northwest Passage to the Indies, something for which Spain and Portugal were beginning to look, the Cabots could claim that, too.

The Northwest Passage did not materialize, but the fishing banks and forests did. The Cabots took possession of them for England in 1497.

Thirty-seven years later, in 1534, Jacques Cartier, equipped with letters of marque from King Francis I of France, crossed the North Atlantic in his turn. The Cabots' landfall had been Cape Breton Island; Cartier's was near the mouth of a great river flowing from the west, which did not turn out to be the Northwest Passage after all but did provide a means of traveling far inland by boat.

The people Cartier encountered were, in the main, fishers and hunters. They raised some grain and vegetables in small gardens tended by their women, but the growing season was short. Here there was no warming Gulf Stream to make intensive agriculture possible in the same latitude as Brittany and England.

Here again there were great forests: pine, oak, maple, and other trees unfamiliar to European eyes. The people dressed in skins; some garments were ornamented with embroidery in porcupine quills, and others were painted. The decorations were simple, and the earth and plant colors were muted—rather drab to eyes accustomed to the brilliant blues of indigo and reds of madder but at least these people had mastered the art of tailoring. Their boots, especially, impressed the French. Knee-high, soft-tanned, and waterproof, hard-soled and lined with fur in winter, or furless in summer, these were the most practical boots for the climate that could have been devised.

The houses of the northeastern peoples were made of wood, the frames of bent boughs set in the ground and covered with mats in winter and bark in summer. Whole clusters of families occupied a single dwelling. It was not until many centuries later that it was determined that each cluster was an "extended family"; that is, descendants of a common ancestor or ancestress.

The weapons these people used were simple: stone-tipped arrows, short bows whose power was reinforced by building up the backs with layers of sinew, and stone-tipped spears and stone knives. Their most complex weapons, aside from the compound bows, were stone- or bone-headed harpoons, which they used in open-water fishing.

Because they were coastal people, these northern Algonkians used canoes: sometimes dugouts, sometimes light frames covered with layers of birchbark. They fished with lines, nets, and the harpoons we have described. Most of their cordage was made from twisted lengths of rawhide or sinew, although sometimes nettle fibers or shredded cedar bark furnished more waterproof cords.

Wood was so abundant in the area that it was used for most household utensils: bowls, spoons, the paddles with which the women stirred boiling maple sap in the spring, and often the troughs into which hot stones were dropped to boil the sap. The women made some coiled pottery, for cooking and storage, but it was simple both in form and in decoration.

There was no gold, silver, or copper in the northeast coastal regions, but wood, fish, and furs were so abundant, and the natives were so willing to trade them for metal knives, needles, and cooking pots, that the land was well worth claiming for France and its growing bourgeois population. Cartier sailed home, well satisfied with what he had found.

Meanwhile, to the south, the struggle between Spain and Portugal for the Caribbean Islands and the mainland to the west of them continued. Launching themselves from bases in the Indies, the conquistadors invaded Mexico, Middle America, and South America. What happened there is germane to what happened to the north only insofar as it provided a later base for Spanish operations.

The first Spanish landfall on the North American continent was Hernando de Soto's sight, in 1539, of the Gulf coast of Florida. Here he landed with an army of six hundred men and at least three women, a walking commissary of pigs, sheep, poultry, and cattle, a pack of greyhounds for hunting, and a herd of lead horses as well as the horses and mules ridden by his followers. He also had with him Franciscan friars. By this time the Inquisition was well under way in Spain, and no opportunity could be overlooked for gathering new souls for the church militant.

At first, as his army moved inland and northward from Tampa Bay, De Soto encountered much the same kind of simple littoral-living people that Columbus had found in the West Indies. In Florida there was no gold, but the people had perfected the arts of working in shell and wood. They knew about pearls, both freshwater and saltwater, and drilled them to wear as ornaments. When these people were asked where wealth came from, they pursed their lips and pointed north.

De Soto continued into what was to become Alabama and Mississippi. Here he encountered an entirely different kind of life. The people lived in stockaded towns, usually set on the second terrace above a river and surrounded by large and fertile fields. Agriculture was much the same as that Cartier had found to the north; corn, beans, and squash formed the basic diet, but here a new plant, of no discernible use except as incense, was grown: tobacco.

Within the stockades the streets were laid out at right angles, and at the east end of each town there was a temple, raised on a pyramidal mound of earth. Like the houses, the temples were built of wattle-daub construction; that is, uprights were set into the ground and willow or dogwood branches were woven back and forth between them, like the wattled cattle sheds of Europe. Over the wattles mud was daubed, and the houses were roofed with thatch of branches and brush. Altogether, the towns presented at least as prosperous and orderly an appearance as the average European village of the period. Many times the outsides and insides of the temples were painted with "heathenish" designs of plumed serpents and winged gods, and carved wooden effigies of the same supernaturals were kept in plaited cane baskets inside the temples, together with whatever treasures of pearls, embossed copper, fine feather-cloth garments, and ornaments of mica and shell the villages possessed.

In a way, De Soto and his followers were impressed by the resemblances between these towns and their places of worship, and those which the Spaniards had reported from conquered central Mexico and the countries south of it. The impression was not false. The Aztecs had sent missionaries on circum-Caribbean expeditions, and these villages were the hinterland of high Mexican civilization, as England and France were the hinterlands of the high Renaissance civilizations of southern Europe.

In other ways the villages reminded the invaders of Mexican towns. Regular areas were set aside for latrine use and for kitchen middens, in each case screened from the village streets and outside the stockades. By Renaissance European standards these Indian villages were almost distressingly clean; even the benches on which people sat or slept were set at least three feet above the floor, or "higher than a flea could jump."

The summer climate in the southeast was hot; spring and fall were mild and pleasant; winters could be cold, especially in the uplands. Therefore the people wore as little as possible in summer; usually breechclouts for the men and small aprons for the women, and added cloaks of dressed skins as the weather grew colder. The nobles wore cloaks of feather cloth, or finely dressed skins embroidered with pearls, and sandals. The common people went barefoot.

This was a class-structured society, like that of Mexico. The nobility, at the top of the social and economic ladder, lived so differently from the farming and laboring classes that it became commonplace among the invaders to speak of "kings" and "slaves," although these terms were not strictly applicable.

Some of the Indians of the southeast were traders whose canoes followed the rivers inland, north and south. They knew of the existence of a great river to the west, and even followed its course northward. The southeasterners traded with the natives, exchanging semiprecious stones for raw copper, among other things. When the traders returned home, they exchanged their imports for other goods.

Among the southeastern Indians there were artists and craftsmen who specialized in carving in wood, bone, shell, and many kinds of semiprecious stones. Amethyst, quartz —both crystalline and colored—garnet, mica sheets, and bauxite were among the minerals they worked. The great art of the southeast was its sculpture.

The women wove baskets from wild cane or from oak or hickory splints. They made and decorated pottery. Here the pottery was hard-fired, thin, and finely decorated with engraving, incising, or painting. Even the "lost wax" process, which was also known in Mexico, was used. Designs were painted on the vessels with beeswax, and the unpainted areas were coated with earth colors. When the vessels were fired, the wax melted and the design remained uncolored—a process of negative painting.

Not only were vessels made for household use and for the storage of seeds and grains; there were also vessels which must have been made specifically for ceremonial use in the temples. Some of these were apparently portraits, perhaps of enemies. There were those that represented heads that had been cut off at the neck; again, perhaps, a dim diffusion of the trophy heads kept in Aztec temples. Sometimes the vessels may have been used in fertility rites, for some that survive are pornographic by twentieth-century judgment. As with all the fine carving, these were probably made by specialists.

Mats were widely used, sometimes as temporary house coverings, sometimes for seats or for tablecloths to be placed on the benches. There were other fabrics, too, besides the famous netted feather cloth, but few descriptions of them have survived.

Impressions left by nets and fabrics used in molding pottery show that plaited cloth was abundant. A characteristic type of pottery, especially cooking and storage vessels, shows that the wet clay was beaten into shape with cord-wrapped paddles, and so the cordage of the area can be determined and described.

Although De Soto's is the most thoroughly documented of the early explorative expeditions, the writers were always men who kept their eyes on the main issue: pearls, semiprecious stones, and the traces of gold that sometimes washed down the mountain streams as the invaders moved northward into what is now Georgia.

The Mobilians, the Biloxi, the Choctaw and Chickasaw, and even the Natchez, whom De Soto's expedition first encountered, were relatively mild and peaceful people. They did not want strangers coming into their lands and looting their temples, but the strangers were equipped with firearms which could outshoot bows and did not hesitate to capture and torture prisoners from the towns that resisted them. Nor did the Spaniards hesitate to set "the tall dogs of Andalusia" on prisoners who attempted to escape. The Indians were defeated by superior technology and they knew it. They ceased to struggle or resist and simply sent the strangers on their way: westward and northward.

Westward and northward lay the hunting and farming lands worked over by the units of the Creek Confederacy: Hitchiti, Muskogee, Alibamu, Koasati, and many others, some of whose names have been lost and forgotten or merged into one single modern political unit in the word Creek.

Like the Choctaw and Chickasaw, the Creek nations spoke a Muskogean language—in fact, the whole linguistic stock derived its name from the principal nation of the Confederacy. These Indians had learned early in their history that in union there is strength, and through the union of small tribes they had come to dominate the area from the middle of Alabama and Mississippi north into the Carolinas.

Creek towns and temples, and in general the people's material way of life, were very similar to those of the more southern tribes. The Creek were more warlike than their neighbors; aggressively warlike. They depended on trade with the Choctaw, particularly, for the niceties of life.

Here De Soto and his army ran into real trouble, for the Creek fought, hard and determinedly, to defend their lands. Spanish horses and cattle were run off, sheep and pigs were stolen and eaten, and a good many of the tall hunting dogs were eliminated by means of Indian arrows.

Still, De Soto and his army were strong enough to recapture most of the horses and to push on northward, into Cherokee country, a people with whom the Creek were sometimes at war, sometimes in a state of uneasy truce and alliances. Opinions among anthropologists differ as to whether the Cherokee were Johnny-come-latelies in the south or represented a remnant group which had remained behind when related tribes moved north.

At any rate, the Cherokee were Iroquoian-speaking; their language was unrelated to any of the Muskogean tongues but was mutually intelligible with those of the Seneca, the Tuscarora, and other members of the northern Iroquoian groups. And the Cherokee had and have the Iroquoian genius for control through political manipulation, for organization, and for government.

Runners went through the Cherokee country, first some sent by the Creek to warn their sometime allies, then trained Cherokee messengers. They traveled by canoe when possible, on foot when they had to leave the waterways for the hills of the Blue Ridge and the beginning of the Allegheny uplift. Word of De Soto's coming spread far and wide before him, and when he and his men reached the Cherokee valley towns they found Indians armed and waiting for them.

This was different country to fight in from the coastal plains and the inland lowlands. The valleys were steep-sided; the hills rushed against the sky and were heavily wooded, with thick underbrush, and the Cherokee had a most unsportsmanlike habit of hiding in the thickets and shooting at the Spaniards before the Spaniards could see them. It was not easy fighting for soldiers trained in the tradition of the Roman Legions, which took for granted an orderly advance across an open plain, a stand-and-deliver technique that permitted the use of firearms by foot soldiers as well as allowing for cavalry charges.

But still there were walled and templed towns; still there were treasures in semiprecious stones and freshwater pearls; and, at last there were measurable traces of gold in the mountain streams. This must be an offshoot of the Eldorado that Cortés had found in Mexico, the Pizarros in Peru; this must be country worth fighting for and conquering, if only those pesky Indians would stand still and fight by the rules, like men!

Driven out of Cherokee country at last, De Soto led his remnant army westward, down the mountain slopes and into the more open alluvial plains between the Alleghenies and the Mississippi. The Spaniards turned southward again, hoping to regain the Gulf coast and its more peaceable inhabitants, and from there to return to Cuba. Most of the horses and dogs were gone by now, and so were the other domesticated animals. Nobody recorded what happened to the women. Clothing was in tatters; armor was stained with rust. Men limped on foot or took turns riding. They threw away their sackfuls of stolen pearls. Their ammunition was nearly exhausted. And now a new rumor reached the struggling invaders. The Indians between them and the Gulf coast were cannibals. They turned westward again and hoped to find the great river. The French said they had found it in the north and that it flowed southward. Perhaps, with canoes, the Spaniards could travel more safely and comfortably downstream to their destination.

They reached the river at last and with great pains, said Rangel, most persistent of their chroniclers. There, perhaps on the riverbank, perhaps out of sight of the flowing water, De Soto died of some strange disease. His men said their Indian guides had poisoned him. More likely he succumbed to the occupational disease of explorers and anthropologists—dysentery reinforced by exhaustion. His men buried him secretly at night, drove their few remaining horses back and forth across the burial place, and continued the heartbreaking struggle back to the coast.

Eventually, after slogging through the cypress swamps and mud of southern Arkansas and northern Louisiana, continually harassed by enemies they could not see and did not try to look for, the Spaniards reached the coast, probably somewhere in the vicinity of Mobile, Alabama. This was not where they had landed, but open water lay before them and across it lay Cuba and comparative civilization. The handful who were left burned and scooped out cypress logs to make canoes and, with their leathern breeches as sails, departed the continent for the safer islands of the Caribbean.

They brought back a surprising amount of information. Towns were described and approximately located; differences in languages were noted, and clothes (especially feather capes and those robes ornamented with pearls) were described with loving care. There was even some attempt to record, through the sheer necessity of dealing with them, the variations in social organization. It was many years before another explorative expedition in North America would be so thoroughly recorded.

3

The Central Vacuum

THE EARLY HISTORY OF THE MISSISSIPPI VALLEY, AND OF some of the larger tributary streams leading into the main one, is tantalizing to archaeologists.

Remains of what is loosely called Archaic culture or cultures are found in caves in bluffs beside streams and have been dated as early as 5000 B.C. The Archaic culture, wherever it occurs on the continent—and we shall make further references to it later—is remarkably homogenous.

The Archaic level is characterized by a knowledge of cordage, netting, and plaiting. Some plaited fabrics in which strands of cord were twined with fur or feathers are known, and there are remains of both plaited rush sandals and hard-soled moccasins. One of the latter, in the Museum of the University of Arkansas, has been resoled nine times, which at least argues that the Archaic women were thrifty and hardworking. There were plaited mats and baskets, made from both cane and rush.

No traces of agriculture have been found in Archaic sites. Wild seeds, and the bones of small game animals which could have been taken in nets or with blowgun darts, are the principal remnants of food found beside the buried fireplaces in the caves. Knives and dart points have been recovered, but no points of those middle sizes which argue a knowledge of the bow or spear.

There was no pottery, as far as we know, in use by the Archaic peoples. They probably wore little clothing except their footgear, but they did some crude carving in shell and bone, and they strung colored seeds to make ornaments. Some burials, usually of infants, have been found in cave floors.

Who these people were, where they came from besides presumably the northwest, and what became of them nobody knows. They were there, and they were gone, but while they lived, the people of the Archaic occupied, at one time or another, most parts of the North American Continent.

About the beginning of the Christian era, other peoples moved into the Mississippi Valley. They were semihorticultural, semihunting, roundheaded individuals. They made and used pottery, and they buried their dead in stone-lined shallow graves, sometimes including with a body the person's treasures in life.

The Adena people, as they are most often called from the first site described, spread along most of the rivers. They had villages and sometimes rush structures that may have served as places of worship. They made pottery and did magnificent carving in stone and bone. Their fabrics and baskets have survived only in fragments because of the dampness of the terrain where most of the Adena people lived.

Down from the north, about A.D. 500, came a wave of invasion. Longheaded, warlike people overran the Adenans. These Hopewellians, as they are called from the town in Ohio where their culture was first described and identified, were great builders of massive effigy mounds. The most famous is the Ohio Serpent Mound, at Hopewell, but effigy mounds in the forms of bears, birds, and semihuman beings are spread throughout Wisconsin, Illinois, and Indiana.

Apparently the effigy mounds were places of worship, not of burial. Few bodies have been recovered from them. In fact, the Hopewellians seem to have made a considerable distinction between the things that are Caesar's and those that are God's. Their villages were seldom located near their ceremonial centers. The latter seem to have been places of worship only, perhaps attended year round by small groups of priest-artists. Horticultural and hunting sites were separately located.

But what craftsmen the Hopewellians were! They made headdresses and ornaments of copper repoussé. They made other ornaments of tenuous sheets of mica. Their pottery was fine and hard, usually engraved or incised with fine-line geometric designs, sometimes with punctate designs of tiny dots, made by indenting the wet clay with a sharp-pointed tool. Often pottery vessels were made in nets, and from the imprints of the fabrics it has been possible to make impressions and reconstruct the weaves of these fossil fabrics.

Characteristic of Hopewell culture are the artifacts known as "boat" and "bird" stones. The bird stones are unmistakable. Their form is that of a bird with wings spread; although they vary in size from a few inches to as much as six across the wingspread, their form is unchanging. Boat stones are keel-shaped, often with flat "decks" as their upper surfaces. Both are made from slate or diorite, stones that can be ground to almost glass-like smoothness.

For many years there was considerable speculation about the uses of boat and bird stones, and the problems are not entirely resolved even now. Many times a hole was drilled through the vertical center of the artifact. It has been speculated that the stones were worn as necklace pendants, carried on staves like banners, or used as weights for spear throwers, or atlatls. The easy way out and the general tendency has been to term them "problematical" objects and let future researchers determine their uses.

Freshwater fish and shellfish formed a large portion of Hopewellian diet, enriched with corn, beans, and squashes and further extended with the meat of large and small game animals. Tobacco must have been grown, for the Hopewell culture is rich in beautifully carved stone pipes and beautifully modeled clay ones. Many show signs of hard and frequent use. Large ceremonial pipes, sometimes with openings for as many as four separate stems, have been recovered. Hopewellian culture was rich and prosperous.

And then, between A.D. 1000 and A.D. 1500, everybody moved out. The Mississippi Valley was depopulated. Many explanations have been advanced: a series of surprise invasions; the termination of a religious cycle which required abandonment of one series of temples and villages and their rebuilding elsewhere—or simply human vagary.

Most likely, however, European-introduced diseases—smallpox, chickenpox, mumps, measles, tuberculosis and the all-too-common cold, to name only a few—were beginning to work their way inland from the coastal fishing villages. With travel along the rivers linking them with the inland villagers, the eastern fishermen could well have begun the spread of epidemics.

At any rate, the Mississippi Valley was an abhorrent vacuum in the middle of the continent almost until systematic European settlement began. And when that settlement did begin, the great heartland of the continent, "the Flanders of America," furnished an ideal dumping ground for Indians who were unwelcome elsewhere.

4

The Vacuum Begins to Fill

THE FIRST PRESSURE AGAINST THE TRIBES OUTSIDE THE Mississippi Valley came from the northeast. De Soto and his shattered army had come and gone, leaving little or no impression, even on the mythology of the southeast.

The French were a different matter. Even before Cartier's landfall at the mouth of the St. Lawrence in 1534, the French could see the commercial possibilities of the New World. Gold and precious stones were not to be despised, but there were other goods here to be exploited. Fishing villages along the Atlantic coast barely touched the harvests that were to be gathered inland.

From the beginning of French contact, the newcomers had traded with the aborigines for furs. The northern pelts were thick, and as fine as the richest of Russian sables. The Indians who brought the furs down to the coast indicated that the source of this wealth lay inland; and inland, following the rivers, went the French.

Europe was torn by wars, both religious and secular. Most of the French explorers had seen military service of one kind or another. They knew how to fight, and they were not averse to fighting, but they did not seek pitched battles with the Indians—trade was too valuable.

In 1517 Martin Luther had pinned his theses to the door of the castle church at Wittenberg. The beginning of Protestantism came less than a century after the invention of printing had made the Word of God, in concrete form, available to all men. Some of the French voyageurs were Huguenots—Protestants—followers of John Calvin, who had expanded Luther's proposals to mean that the Word of God was also the Word of Man's Freedom. But the majority of the French were Catholics, and the Jesuit priests who accompanied trading parties kept them so.

In 1534 the Renaissance was ending in Europe, pausing briefly in England, and remaining on the eastern shore of the Atlantic. It scarcely touched North America except in the brief, inglorious episode of De Soto in the southeast and the invasion by Coronado of the southwest. Eastern North America was settled—under royal patents, to be sure—by the rising bourgeoisie, the businessmen of the new cities that were rising and spreading all over the continent.

This was especially true with the men who came from overpopulated France and England. Royalty and nobility had taken over vast agricultural acreages to make parks and hunting grounds. The lowest classes lived from the land, one step above starvation, or sought their fortunes in the cities. There was an increasing demand for skilled craftsmen. The expropriation of forests had also created a need for timber. Shipwrights and millworkers found themselves unemployed because of the lack of raw materials with which to work.

North America was rich in raw materials, if in nothing else. French explorers began moving inland, to see how far this wealth extended. Along the St. Lawrence, the Illinois, the Ohio, they traveled, always accompanied by the specially trained Jesuit priests who had been hardened physically to endure their missionary experiences. At last La Salle reached clear and open water—the Gulf of Mexico, into which the Mississippi poured.

La Salle's expedition was almost as well recorded as De Soto's. Little was written in his secretary's accounts concerning the lower Mississippi tribes, unfortunately. We know that most of the Indians there were Caddoan-speaking, but we do not know exactly how numerous the groups were or what their social organization was. There seems to have been a loose confederation among the eastern Caddoan bands, around the Texas Gulf. Possibly this had been derived from the organization of their eastern neighbors, the Creek. There is a linguistic link between Caddoan languages and the Cherokee Iroquoian, although not with Muskogean, but how strong and immediate this link originally had been no one knows.

Non-Caddoan tribes of the lower Mississippi Valley included the Tonkawa and the Karankawa. Both were noted for their ceremonial cannibalism. They may have furnished one outpost of Aztec culture north of the Gulf of Mexico.

In general, the lower Mississippi tribes were semihorticultural and the Caddo, particularly, were noted farmers. Small game was abundant in the Texas-Louisiana area, and mule deer ran in the dense thickets. Farther west, the Wichita lived on the margin between the true plains and the cross timbers, and were buffalo hunters as well as farmers.

Houses were square or round, thatched with bundles of straw and sometimes daubed with mud, sometimes left with air spaces among the bundles. They ranged in size from the simple square low-roofed and porched farmhouses of the Nadakao, Tawakoni, and Kichai to the great round domed structures of the Wichita.

Like most horticulturalists, the Caddoans made both pottery and basketry. They wore little clothing: one-piece moccasins, simple breechclouts or aprons, and robes of soft-tanned deerskin in cold weather.

The Caddoans and their neighbors were canoe people, and good fishermen. Remains of their cypress dugouts have been recovered from the Louisiana swamps. Possibly they used the canoes for hunting muskrats, which were abundant, and beavers, which were slightly less so, as well as for fishing.

These people were most easily exploited, however, as human beings. Captives could be sold as slaves into the developing Spanish colonies around the Caribbean, and the name of one of the more northern Caddoan tribes, the Pawnee, became synonymous with "slave" to French and Spanish alike. Indian prisoners did not survive long or breed well in captivity, however. Their economically productive life-span was only three or four years, so frequent raids for more slaves were necessary. This had the ultimate effect of practically depopulating the lower Mississippi Valley.

Further progress inland was blocked, beyond the western alluvial plain, by two factors. The first of these was the belt of cross timbers, a dense growth of scrub oak, pin oak, and blackjack, lashed together by brambles and other dense underbrush. It was generally agreed that the cross timbers, from the Texas coast to the Missouri Ozarks, were impassible. Not even trails led through these woodlands, except along the streams.

Another barrier to westward exploration was the Arkansas River's Great Raft. For nearly a hundred miles upstream from the river's confluence with the Mississippi there extended a solid logjam, mostly of small wood washed down from the cross timbers to the west but packed hard enough for a man to walk on. Navigation upstream on the Arkansas, the main southern tributary to the Mississippi, was out of the question. So what lay to the west of the river remained, in the southern part of its course, a mystery that endured almost two hundred years after La Salle's voyage.

Obviously, then, we know more about the tribes of the north central area than of the south central. Inland from the Atlantic, for more than a thousand miles, to and around the Great Lakes, cultures differed little from those of the coast except in more dependence on meat and less on fish in the diet.

The strongest, and certainly the best known, of the northeastern groups was the Iroquois Confederacy. Its units controlled the area from Lake Erie to the Atlantic and dominated the Algonquian-speaking tribes from Hudson Bay to the Ohio River.

The Iroquois spoke of their heartland, in the center of this vast stretch of country, as their Longhouse, in which each tribe occupied a definite position. This was a deliberate correlation with the longhouses in which the Iroquois resided: vast vaulted structures of planks on wooden frameworks. Trees were cut and planks were riven with stone and wooden tools. In all parts of their lives the Iroquois thought in terms of wood, and they were superb workers in the substance. They alone, probably, of all American Indian tribes, had some understanding of the Europeans' need and desire for wood.

The Iroquois equated their religion, too, with the Great Tree from which the tribes sprang as branches. As each branch is supported by and supports the growth of the main trunk, so each division of the Iroquois Confederacy —the Seneca, Cayuga, Onondaga, Oneida, and Mohawk —drew strength from the others.

Iroquoian unity opposed the British but made alliance with the French. Until the Revolutionary War, the Iroquois held the balance of power between New France and the English colonies. Expert diplomats and deft political machine men, the Iroquois remained a force to be reckoned with for centuries.

As the Europeans moved in from the Atlantic, so the Iroquois moved westward and southward, pushing before them the Algonkian tribes with whom they had already made alliances or whom they had put under subjugation. So the coastal Delaware found themselves building villages along the Ohio and Wabash rivers, and tribes like the Sauk and Fox and Potawatomi, long settled in the area of the Great Lakes, began moving south to the Rock and Illinois rivers, and farther westward across the Mississippi. The vacuum was beginning to fill.

5

What Filled the Vacuum?

THE TRIBES THAT MOVED INTO THE MISSISSIPPI VALLEY ahead of the Iroquois drive shared many traits in common with each other and with the Iroquoians.

All were semihorticultural, semihunting peoples. They used houses with rectangular floor plans, of varying sizes; from the Iroquois apartment houses, which could and did accommodate a nuclear family, its descendants, and its collateral relatives such as uncles and aunts and their families, to the single-family dwellings preferred by the Kickapoo. As we move southward, the houses become smaller and more compact. Planks are replaced by cattail mats, the stems stitched together with bone needles. Furniture remains the same: benches along the walls, with plaited rush mats thrown over them.

Some pottery was made by the Algonquian-speaking tribes of the Great Lakes and middle Mississippi region into historic times, but it remained crude and relatively undecorated. What is sometimes called "secondary primitivity" set in; what had been skillfully made in an early period now deteriorated in craftsmanship and aesthetics.

Among the Algonkians there were skillfull carvers in wood and stone, and much of their sculpture compares favorably with Iroquoian work in the same materials.

The great craft of the Great Lakes and Mississippi Valley peoples of the discovery period, however, was textile making. This was not loom weaving, but finger weaving. Plaited, twined, and netted fabrics were produced. Designs had great flexibility and lightness. They included animal and human figures, as well as geometric forms and semblances of curves.

The religious and social systems of the Iroquois were closely integrated with one another; in fact, it would not be too much to say that they often were one and the same. The Iroquois accorded a position of considerable importance to women; women did not speak or vote in councils, but they held the power of veto.

Among the Algonkians there was less formality in social structure and less rigidity in religion. The family and clan were the basic Algonkian units, and from them developed a series of social and economic requirements and sanctions.

Iroquoian clans were matrilineal; Lewis Henry Morgan, the first serious student of North American Indian ethnology, went so far as to speak of Iroquoian "matriarchy," although that statement seems a little exaggerated. At least, the Iroquois reckoned descent through the mother rather than the father, and a woman had as much right to divorce her husband as he had to leave her or take another wife. The house and household possessions belonged to the woman; a man owned only his tools, his weapons, and the few clothes he stood up in.

Our information about Algonkian clans is less clear than that on the Iroquoian. Probably these clans, too, were originally matrilineal. Certainly the women owned their houses, their furniture, and their children, while an Algonkian man was in the same situation as an Iroquois, as far as material possessions went.

Trade goods certainly came into this area in 1534, and the material culture changed rapidly as beads, cloth, steel knives and needles, brass kettles, axes and hammers and adzes, were exchanged for furs. Tomahawks were introduced by the Europeans and copied by the Indians for added convenience in making both peace and war.

We should be hard pushed to know the little we do about the central peoples if it had not been for a provision that was uniformly written into the charters of French trading companies. Each corporation was required, annually, to return to France samples of the works of the Indians with whom its employees came in contact. These objects would be used for the education of the dauphins, so that future kings of France might know what manner of men inhabited their overseas dominions.

All these artifacts, dutifully sealed in lead chests and returned to France, accumulated and gathered dust in the attics of the Tuileries Palace from 1536 until the fall of the French monarchy. Whether any king of France ever laid eyes on the chests' contents is doubtful, for the whole vast store was quickly forgotten.

In the early 1930's somebody was moved to do a thorough spring housecleaning of the Tuileries storage areas. The chests were uncovered and opened, then shut tight and hidden again during Hitler's conquest of France. When France became once more an autonomous nation, the Indian collection was brought to light again and became the basis of the present Musée de l'Homme, in Paris.

So much for the whims of rulers and the quirks of fate. It is an anthropological truism that when two cultures encounter, the superior material traits of each will be absorbed by the other. The French learned to eat corn and beans and squash, and the Indians learned to use metal tools, implements, and weapons. Neither culture would ever be the same again after the encounter.

Interestingly enough, throughout their history each Algonkian tribe seems to have had a balance tribe. As in their internal moiety systems, where each clan had a sister clan, with reciprocal responsibilities, so, outside the tribe, there was a sister tribe. Always the alliances were between hunting people, like the Fox, and farming people, like the Sauk. The pairing might even extend to a tribe of another linguistic stock; the Algonkian Ojibwa were paired with the Siouan Winnebago, for instance.

In the case of women's crafts, the change after the French traders entered the area was particularly striking. Who wanted to bother laboriously coiling and smoothing pottery, when there were brass kettles to be had? The kettles would hold as much food at a time as the pottery vessels, or more; they were lighter and easier to carry when the village went on a hunt; they were far more durable. Pottery ceased to be.

Basketry and mats continued to be made, for there were no adequate imported substitutes. Woolen and cotton fabrics replaced tanned hides for clothing, although belts, garters, and some ornamental strips for leggings and shirts were still made by the finger-weaving process.

The most dramatic change was the substitution of beads for porcupine quills in embroidery. The beads were more brightly colored, more uniform in size, and easier to work with. Designs became increasingly florid and flowery, reflecting the curves of the branches and the plants of the surrounding woodland world. Whole books can be and have been written about the different kinds of beads introduced by Europeans, their places of manufacture on the continent, and their effect on American Indian art styles. It is enough to say here that glass beads were not made by any American Indians until much later than the date when trading began, and then only in a single instance, that of the Mandan.

There were inevitable changes in religions. As the tribes were pushed closer together, and began to exchange ideas as well as goods, religions combined and separated, grew upon and into one another, and underwent the same kinds of changes that social and economic institutions did. Underlying all North American Indian religions there seems to have been a basic pattern: a Supreme Being and a Creator who were sometimes but not necessarily the same, with a host of attendant nature spirits who personified the earth, the sun, moon and stars, plants, birds, animals, flowers, and trees. The Sauk and Fox both say that the trees had clans, and that there was a "chief tree," but its identity is lost in the forests of time.

Also, the impact of Christianity must be considered. As has been said, every trading and exploring group included priests or ministers as a matter of course. In the early years of "discovery and exploration" the Roman Catholics predominated, the Jesuits accompanying the French, and the Franciscans and Dominicans the Spaniards.

Eastern and southern tribes, especially the Siouans and Caddoans, had begun sifting into the Mississippi Valley even before the French push from the northeast drove the Iroquoians inland and forced the Algonkians to move westward ahead of the newcomers.

Northward from the mouth of the Mississippi into its central valley, and along such main tributary streams as the White, the Red, the St. Francis, and the Brazos, the people lived much as their more northern neighbors did. There was one exception; a westward extension of the southern mound-building cultures reached as far as western Arkansas and eastern Oklahoma and Texas. The relationship—if relationship there was—between these peoples, their southeastern contemporaries, and the tribes known to have occupied the area in historic times is yet to be worked out.

We can safely say that the historic movement into the Mississippi Valley is mappable—one hundred miles every ten years was the usual rate of drift. Absorbing new culture traits, abandoning old ones, changing and shifting without consciousness of doing so, the Indians moved into what was later to be called "the Flanders of America" because of its richness of soil and easy accessibility.

It is small wonder that the contemporary descendants of these peoples have little sense of the passage or value—to non-Indians—of time. "A long time ago" may mean a lifetime, a century, or six weeks. "To keep Indian time" means to be always slow in meeting appointments. The sense of urgency behind each move telescoped days and years until they were indistinguishable one from another.

6

The Northward Movements

IT IS A TEMPTATION TO CALL THIS CHAPTER "MEANWHILE, Back at the Ranch," for with the northward invasion of the Spanish conquerors of Mexico two great new factors entered the American southwest: horses and cattle. What was to become famous as ranching country entered on its new career.

The Spanish conquest of Mexico was quick and complete. The Aztec government centered in one man, who was both religious and secular head of his people: Moctezuma. When he was captured and killed, when his nephew and successor, Cuauhtémoc, had been put to death, the tribes the Aztecs had subdued had little or no interest in opposing a new set of conquerors. The Spaniards took over the country, partitioned it into great estates, established a central government in the former Aztec capital, Tenochtitlán, now Mexico, D.F., and then looked around to see what came next. Middle America, the Caribbean Islands, and much of South America were under Spanish or Portuguese control already. There was nowhere to go but north.

Out of the north came word that the country there was worth exploring. In about 1523 Cabeza de Vaca and his Moorish slave, Estevan, had been shipwrecked on the Texas Gulf coast. With incredible efforts they crossed the Sonora desert and toiled southward along the Sierra Madre into Mexico, to reach the capital and report the existence of seven great cities of Cibola, richer by far than any city in Mexico. With Estevan as a guide—the slave had been reverenced by the Indians he had met and was anxious to return to his prestigious state—an expedition, under Francisco Vásquez de Coronado, was organized and set out in 1540.

Coronado's was purely a military and exploring expedition. He was interested first in gold and jewels, then in salable slaves, and, finally, in land. With him he took a well-equipped and armed and orderly body of troops, enough stock to feed them on the way, and no women. Women could be had for the taking in Indian communities, as the Spaniards already had learned in Mexico.

Estevan was sent ahead of the main body of troops, with instructions that he was to send back crosses commensurate with the size of the treasures he found. The returning crosses, some small and some large, must have done much to preserve the morale of the troops as they slogged their way through the northern Mexican deserts, from water hole to water hole. At last a cross of enormous size arrived. Coronado pushed on, but when he came upon Estevan it was to find the former slave lolling like a Roman emperor among such poor luxuries as the mud-walled pueblos of Zuni could provide. Estevan was disposed of promptly, by the Zunis, and Coronado got down to the serious business of exploring.

The Indians whom the Spaniards met in the sixteenth century had come into the southwest about the beginning of the Christian era. They fall into two main divisions: the ancestral Anasazi, from whom are descended the Pueblo Indians we know today, and the ancestral Hohokam, from whom are descended the Yuman groups, the Mohave, and the Pima and Papago.

The two ancestral groups had certain things in common: they were horticulturalists, who depended on their fields for their main subsistence; they made pottery and baskets; and they were textile makers. Each sprang from the Archaic base we have already mentioned as existing throughout the continent. But in many ways they were widely different.

Beginning about A.D. 300 the Anasazi had begun building cities in the Four Corners area, where Arizona, Colorado, New Mexico, and Utah join. Such centers as the communities which were clustered on the Mesa Verde, Colorado, and at Aztec, New Mexico, show a people with a highly developed material culture, a well-established ceremonialism, and a horticulture that was sufficiently flourishing to support such luxuries as priests and artists.

About A.D. 1200 drought, as we know from our old friends the tree rings, descended on the southwest. The country became inhospitable in the extreme, and the people of the Four Corners moved southward, to establish such communities as Casa Grande, Arizona; Pueblo Bonito, New Mexico, and the ancestral Hopi villages. Along the Rio Grande and its tributaries, and along the upper Colorado, walled cities built around central plazas came into being.

Simultaneously with the drought, or a short time before it, a wave of invasion into the southwest began from the northwest. The Athabascan peoples of the Columbia and Mackenzie rivers, whose basic culture was still very much like that of the Archaic, began raiding southward. It may be because of the Apache and Navaho, as we know them, or Dené (the People), as they call themselves, that *toreones*, or watchtowers, were built and occupied in the Galisteo river basin, in northern New Mexico, and that the walls of villages were made of houses joined solidly together for defense.

Anasazi culture spread along the Rio Grande, as far south as the river went. Where the bend to the east began, Anasazi culture ended. Westward Anasazi culture extended as far as central Arizona and northeastward to Pecos Pueblo on the border of the Great Plains. Anasazi culture was and remains surprisingly homogeneous, wherever it is located.

Outside the village lie the fields which the men cultivate. The ever-present American triad—corn, beans, and squash—is planted, together with tobacco and sunflowers, the latter as a source of both food oils and dye colors.

In the Rio Grande and other comparatively well-watered areas, the fields are located near the villages. The Hopi of north-central Arizona, where water is a scarce and seasonal thing, plant above the seep springs of the desert. An entire cornfield may be the size of a dining room table. The corn grows two or three feet high but has deep and wide-spreading root systems that absorb every drop of moisture. It is still not uncommon for a Hopi farmer to make a round of twenty-five miles a day to tend all his fields.

Within the village is the plaza, and in the plaza are the *kivas*, as the Hopi call them. The other villagers have accepted and use this word. These gathering places for the men of the town are part religious, part educational, part workshops. Preparations for ceremonies go on in the kivas; boys are trained in men's ways and works, and spinning and weaving of cotton, both men's crafts, are often done in the kivas in winter. Women are not entirely excluded but are admitted as spectators—and sometimes as participants—in certain ceremonies.

Each village is divided into moieties, or halves; one of the summer, one of the winter, people. Each moiety has its own great kiva. Within the moieties are the clans, with descent reckoned through an individual's mother. The clans, in turn, have smaller kivas. In her house each woman sets up a small shrine to the domestic gods, so that religion was and is, to the Anasazi and their descendants, an integral part of daily life. Children are taught their clan and moiety identifications as they are taught their names, for the larger identifications are fixed and unchanging, while a name can be altered.

In the Pueblos, the dominant figure in each family is the mother's oldest brother. He is responsible for the lives and behavior of his sisters' children; to him they go for instruction, council, and comfort, and it is their uncle who inflicts punishment on bad children.

The father of the family is held in affectionate regard, but he and his brothers and sisters are not members of one's *own* family. They are members of their mother's family and take the same responsibility toward their siblings' children that the mother's brother does toward his. Father may correct, but he may not punish, his own children; he may advise, but he may not counsel. Authority is in his relationship to the children of his sisters.

A household, then, consists of a woman, her married daughters, and their children. Husbands live with their wives but in the wives' houses, from which they may be ejected. In that case, the man returns to his own mother's or sister's dwelling, for it is his clan home, and his place is with the clan before it is with the nuclear family.

As a woman's family grows, rooms may be added for the new descendants. A house or a room may be bequeathed by the mother of the family to a child or grandchild, and it is only in such cases of inheritance that men own the roofs over their heads.

The men, on the other hand, use and work the fields. Nobody, of course, *owns* land in our sense, but the village council assigns land to each man to meet his needs and those of his family. The individual plots are part of the larger clan and moiety properties, and if, for any reason, a man does not work or use his land, it reverts to his ancestral groups or is reassigned to his nephews.

Women usually are present at planting ceremonies, which are small, private observances held when the time is right for putting the seed into each plot of earth. While the men plant the first seeds with digging sticks like those the men of the Anasazi used, the women, shawl-shrouded and secretive, huddle at the edge of the field and softly sing encouragement to men and seed alike, for men and seed are one, and without women they will not bring forth any fruit.

From the time that the seed is in the ground, the men alone work the fields, with the exception of the small bean fields, or "women's gardens," that are planted near the houses. These are the housewife's care. She may also own individual fruit trees and vines, some of them a day's walk from her house.

As soon as a crop is harvested and brought home, it becomes no longer a man's, but his wife's. She is responsible for the preservation and preparation of food, and so the crops pass into her hands. She may divide the food with her husband's family, and most women do so, but there is no rule that crops must be shared.

Each house is provided with storerooms, sometimes separate from the family living quarters and sometimes incorporated with them. A share of each crop is placed in the hands of the village council, for distribution to widows, orphans, and visitors. The remainder is stowed in the storerooms.

Ideally, each family should have four years' supply of food on hand. The storeroom should be emptied every autumn, the previous crops moved forward, and the latest harvest stacked on shelves or hung from the rafters or poured into pottery storage jars along the back wall. Actually, of course, the ideal is seldom met nowadays. The introduction of canned foods in grocery stores, of home freezers and of supermarkets along highways, have changed all that. Even so, a thrifty Pueblo housewife dries a part of each year's harvest and stores it in the old way —just in case.

Things have changed in some ways in the Pueblos since Coronado's time, but many of the roots of social and religious life went deep, and while the institutions that grew from them aboveground may have been bent, they have not been broken.

Essentially, Pueblo life was and is theocratic. The true

head of the community, usually called today by the Aztec name, *cacique,* is the ruling priest. He is much too important and sacred a person to deal with outsiders, and is represented by an ambassador or spokesman, now known as the *governor.* In all public functions the governor appears as the voice of the cacique and also as the voice of the village. This has given Pueblo governors, to non-Pueblo eyes, an importance they have never actually enjoyed.

Assisting the governor in secular affairs are the *war captains,* or *lieutenants.* Theirs is the responsibility today of parking visitors' cars outside the plazas on feast days, or even of excluding visitors altogether when a ceremony is too esoteric for non-Pueblo eyes. The war captains collect camera fees or destroy forbidden cameras and notebooks. Like the governor, the captains are front men, expressing the will and the wish of the cacique to the outside world. No doubt Coronado was greeted by the sixteenth-century equivalents of these men when he first entered Zuni, for the cacique of that day must certainly have remained concealed behind the scenes.

Age has little to do with the cacique's authority, but his training is all-important. From earliest childhood, the boy who will inherit this position, through his mother's line, is specially taught in the kiva, by his predecessor and by the other priests. In some villages, where a cacique has died before his successor could be trained, the new holder of priesthood has been sent elsewhere, so that his training could be completed by the men with the proper knowledge. The cacique is a priest and a scholar; a generous, kind, and good man, who does not hoard material possessions for himself and his family but who shares willingly with those who are in need. He is, in many ways, above and beyond human power and authority, and is one who communes directly with the supernaturals.

We can speak of these institutions in the present tense, because they do exist today. Not that the Pueblos and their organizations are living museums, but because these people reverence their past and have a profound understanding of the continuity of time. "Time was, and is, and always will be," a Pueblo priest said once. "It flows like a river; it does not stand still like lakes. That is what we Indians know, and you have never learned."

He spoke truth, for the children learn what their grandparents know. Ideally, they continue it. In actual practice, this is not always possible.

Both religion and ceremonialism are highly developed

among the Pueblo Indians. The yearly cycle begins in the winter, with the December solstice. It continues a round of fertility; hunting dances until the mountain snows melt; planting and growing dances in the spring and early summer; harvest dances in the autumn. A "dance," in Pueblo concept, is a religious pageant, the acting-out of the spirit of the given season.

And so it was—time flowing backward, now—when Coronado invaded the southwest. Both he and his missionaries were shocked by the "heathenish practises" they observed in village plazas. No doubt the acting-out of fertility rites was even more graphic then than it is now, and even today it can be shocking by conservative twentieth-century standards. But why anyone familiar with the Spanish vice-regal courts should not have been shock-proof beggars the imagination.

Be that as it may, Coronado and the Franciscan and Dominican friars who accompanied him decided that these were *"gentes sin raison"*—people without reason or souls—whose lack should be immediately supplied. Wholesale baptisms—whole villages at a time—took place. Each Indian received a Spanish name, which was to replace his own. Each village was renamed for a Spanish saint, who became its protector. Some villages, like the central Tewa; San Ildefonso, San Juan, Santa Clara, and others, accepted the changed nomenclature outwardly. Others, like Taos, Zia, Acoma, Zuni, and the Hopi towns, rejected the new names.

Nor did all villages meekly submit to the Spanish baptisms. In Zuni there was outright rebellion, and the Spaniards were driven out finally. The Hopi—People of Peace, as they call themselves, or not—took even more direct action by slinging the priests over the five-hundred-foot drops of the cliffs at Awatobi and Oraibi. But by and large, the Pueblo Indians conformed to Spanish wishes—outwardly.

Coronado and his troops spent their first winter north of Mexico proper at the large pueblo of Kuauwa, which is now Coronado State Monument, New Mexico, north and west of Bernalillo. It was not an easy time for anybody. The troops were quartered on the Indians; the Indians objected and retaliated by cutting down on food supplies.

All winter long, the leading men of the village, with a stubborn consistency, argued with Coronado that the Seven Cities of Cibola lay, in Spanish phrase, *mas alla*—farther on, to the east. In spring, with the troops and horses tired and out of condition from the hard winter, Coronado moved on, first to Pecos Pueblo and then farther east, onto the margin of the Great Plains.

There they met the western Caddoans, the Wichita, living in villages, it is true, but in villages made up of clusters of thatched houses that in no way resembled the great cities of Mexico. *Cíbola*—buffalo—they found in abundance, and sent back detailed reports and drawings of the "great shaggy cattle" of the Plains. But wealth, no.

It was a disheartened band of explorers who returned to Pecos and Kuauwa. Only the missionary priests asked permission to remain in the northern country, and Coronado and the rest of the army returned along the Jornado del Muerto (Dead Man's Road) that paralleled the Rio Grande and then crossed the northern Mexican desert, to the capital.

Coronado did bring back reports of great open meadows, suitable for grazing horses and other livestock; of mountains that *might* contain treasures of gold, silver, and precious stones if they were properly explored; and of a peaceful agricultural population, hospitable when urged to be and submissive when forced. Here was land for occupancy. Why let a few corn-planting Indians stand in the way of Spanish development of haciendas?

A series of semimilitary, semiexplorative *entradas*, modeled on Coronado's, followed. All were aimed at defining the limits of the new country and mapping it while, of course, converting the Indians to Christianity. A few attempts at colonization were made, but none was effective until that of Juan de Oñate, in 1598.

Oñate took with him not only military personnel and the requisite number of priests. He took married men and their wives; he took rams and ewes; stallions and mares, and burrows; bulls and cows. This time the Spaniards had come to stay.

In addition to breeding livestock, Oñate took the root stocks of such European trees as apples, pears, apricots, figs, nectarines, and wine grapes. Chokecherries, wild currants, and gooseberries already grew in abundance along the streams, but the colonists brought raspberries and European blackberries, and asparagus.

An inventory of Oñate's expedition reads like the prize list in the agricultural division at a state fair. It included wheat, rye, and barley, for the Europcans were not yet sure that they could sustain life on the native maize, beans, and squashes. For good measure, the colonists included chili peppers and tomatoes, for which they had acquired a taste in Mexico, and both onions and garlic, for most of the native herbs would be unfamiliar to them. Naturally, the colonists were provided with two-wheeled carts drawn by draft oxen, in which they transported their agricultural implements as well as their seed and root stock.

At the junction of the Chama and the Rio Grande stood a large pueblo called Yunqueyunque in Tewa, San Juan de los Caballeros in Spanish nomenclature. Here the people had already proved more than usually hospitable to strangers, and here Oñate established his capital. Whether the village was named St. John of the Knights because of the good manners of its occupants or because they took readily to horse breeding and training is still a matter of some question. Both statements are true. Horse breeding in North America began at San Juan, and it was probably strays from the San Juan herds, sifting northward and eastward, who provided the basis for a later culture, that of the Great Plains.

Spanish control of New Mexico continued and spread for almost a hundred years, growing increasingly highhanded in the process. At last, in 1680, the Indians could stand it no longer. A man from San Juan, Popé, established a base of operations at Taos and from there sent messengers to the other villages. Each man carried a string in which were tied knots to mark the number of days until all should rise against the Spaniards. It was the first, and almost the only, concerted movement of American Indians against Europeans.

The signal for attack was given too soon in some villages. Spanish settlers who had made themselves liked by the Indians were warned of the impending danger. Some of them escaped, others warned their compatriots, and New Mexico was retaken by the Indians only at a high price in lives and property. The Spanish settlers recrossed the Rio Grande and found refuge in the small communities that had grown up in northern Mexico since Coronado's time.

Indian control of the southwest continued from 1680 to 1692, when Diego Francisco de Vargas, carrying with him a specially blessed and dedicated figure of the Virgin of Compostella, reentered the territory, and with the aid of *La Conquistadora,* as the Virgin was known, subdued it again. This time he did not risk establishing the capital city near a large and active Pueblo, but chose the site of a small, poor one which could easily be moved aside. There he built Santa Fe, still the capital of New Mexico, following plans sent out from Seville for the walling and protection of Spanish colonial towns, and there he built the first church, north of Mexico, in the Indian barrio which, with the church, he named San Miguel. The building is still standing and is occasionally used for religious services. It has been repaired and restored, and it is now a state monument.

Later a larger church, dedicated to St. Francis of Assisi—perhaps for the further increase of flocks and herds—was constructed, and *La Conquistadora* found her permanent home in what is now the Cathedral of St. Francis. Once a year, on the feast of the Virgin of Guadalupe, patron saint of all Indians, *La Conquistadora* leaves her shrine in the cathedral and is carried in state to the Indian quarter of the city, where she passes a week in the Church of Guadalupe and is then ceremonially returned to her home.

"Time was, time is, time will be." No one can think or write of, let alone live among, the Pueblos, without being impressed with the depth of truth of that statement. Religion and many ceremonies have "gone underground" and are hidden from prying eyes, but they are there. The great myths are told. The people live within their walls, guarding their privacy as best they may, and it is the rare non-Indian who penetrates within the walls of even a private house.

Nor are the Spanish villages very greatly changed from the life of the sixteenth century. The woman who proudly exhibits her *"casa moderno de seexty-foor,"* designed and constructed from the pages of women's magazines purchased in a supermarket, is the wife of a carver of wooden santos—those figures of the saints that bless all Spanish-American homes. Her husband's figure of San Pascual, patron saint of the kitchen and good cooks, stands in a niche in the adobe wall above her liquid-petroleum-fired kitchen range.

Here, if anywhere in the United States, the problem of coexistence of cultures—Indian, Spanish, and the later Anglo-American—has been worked out to a reasonably peaceable conclusion. Neither the Indians nor the Spanish-Americans are usually people of great wealth. They do not desire to be, although every new usable culture trait is desired and treasured.

Agriculture and stock breeding may have been introduced, but native horticulture continues. House and village plans are much the same, whatever the population group. Houses, churches, and some public buildings are still built of adobe, or of concrete block disguised to look like adobe construction.

Generally speaking, in spite of villages that were wiped out, and others that moved to and incorporated themselves with larger ones, the Indians of the southwest simply moved over to accommodate the newcomers and then continued in their old patterns. Trade goods improved their lives materially. New foods were added to their diets. But the Pueblo Indians were dedicated to being peaceable, and they stubbornly continued to act that way—most of the time.

It is easy to make the picture too idyllic, to come down with what one visitor has called "a bad case of quaints." And it is most important to remember, in speaking and writing of the Indians of the Rio Grande drainage, that peaceful coexistence was not easily or peacefully attained and that its continuance is still a matter of uncertainty and doubt.

Nor can one overlook the darker side of Pueblo Indian life. There are evil witches, as well as beneficent spirits and blessed saints. All the world is divided, black and white, weak and strong, light and dark, good and bad. One is as certain to exist as the other.

A Hopi woman commented on the unusual number of deaths of children in another village: "Well, what can you expect? Those people over there are witches, most of them. Every time they use bad power to hurt someone else, one of their own children dies." It was a matter-of-fact statement, as businesslike as the following one: "I won't let my husband go over there to trade. He and my brother are the only ones I have left, and I don't want to take any chances." A sigh. "They pay good prices for peaches in that village, though. I sure hate to lose that business, but I don't want to risk it."

A deserted house may be observed to glow with an unearthly blue light at night, on the outskirts of a Rio Grande village. "It's the witches' kiva, and they are holding their meetings when you see that light. Don't ever go near it." Or a woman from one village, visiting another's fiesta may refuse to leave her car. "There are witches there, and if you step on their earth, they can get you." None of these speakers was an ignorant or unsophisticated person. Simply, they had grown up with witches; evil deeds as well as good ones are part of life and are accepted as of human existence.

The power of a known witch may be negated, to som extent, by avoidance. But the witch, hiding in the dark, may catch a victim on the way to the outhouse or going to visit a neighbor. In that case, the victim is ridden like a horse to the witches' kiva and there is forced to become one of the coven. His only way of escape is through finding someone with healing power, usually the cacique, who can and will drive out the evil spirit and turn him free. Pueblo Indians, except the young men who have taken to drinking, seldom go out at night.

So life seesaws back and forth within and without the Pueblo walls. Good and evil war against each other, and there is no victory for either, for they are evenly matched.

As the walls of the houses protect the village, and bond it in a unit, so the lives of families are a bond and a protection for the individual members. Only if the people of the family and of the village stand together can anyone be safe.

7

The Engineers

IF THE ORDER OF THIS BOOK WERE STRICTLY CHRONOlogical, we should be forced to skip from New Mexico and Arizona to the California coast and the voyages of Sir Francis Drake. But geography also imposes rules and order. It seems best to remain a few chapters longer within the limits of the southwest and to describe the other kinds of life that were lived there.

South of the Anasazi, in the drainages of the lower Colorado, the Gila, and the Salt rivers, the aboriginal dwellers were also peoples of high culture. Today they are known by a Piman word, the Hohokam—those who have gone before.

The Hohokam were strongly influenced by the Mexican cultures to the south of them. They built cities, with central plazas and great ball courts (the one at Snaketown, Arizona, is 160 by 81 feet). The ballgame played in these arenas, with sloping sides for seats, must have been similar to Aztec games, for rubber balls, presumably made in British Honduras, have been excavated from the courts.

Avenues led through the cities, joining ball courts and temples, although few people seem to have lived in these communities the year round. The bulk of the Hohokam population appears to have lived outside the villages, in the small communities the Spanish were later to refer to as *rancherias.*

Among the Hohokam were skilled workers in shell and stone inlays. These artists had also learned to etch designs on shells by using acid from soured cactus juice. The art of metal casting had reached the point of making copper bells by the lost wax process. Similar bells have been recovered from sites in Middle America and Mexico.

Hohokam pottery reached a high point in decorative art, and a technical versatility all its own. Other North American Indian wares were made by laboriously coiling ropes of pottery and placing them one upon another to form a vessel. The coils were joined and smoothed by rubbing with stones, shells, or pieces of gourd shell, and decoration was applied to the finished piece.

Among the Hohokam, the paddle-and-anvil method of pottery making was developed. The potter shaped a lump of clay between her hands, punched a hole in the top with her fist, and then paddled the outside of the vessel with a flat wooden implement while holding a flat stone against the inside wall as an anvil. This was no less laborious a process than the coil method, but it did produce a wider variety of forms.

The Hohokam potters produced clay figurines which are strongly suggestive of Aztec votive figures. Sometimes these were sunbaked; sometimes they were fired. The figurines that have been found in archaeological sites are so numerous as to suggest that they may have been individual tokens of power.

Along the Mimbres River, in southwestern New Mexico, a Hohokam-derived culture developed, called today the Mimbres culture. Like the dwellers in the more western Hohokam communities in Arizona, the Mimbres people lived in pit houses, constructed half underground. Each house was entered by a long tunnel from the east and was thatched with grass reinforced with packed clay. The shape of the pit houses was that of an Eskimo igloo.

Pit houses had characterized one phase of Anasazi culture, and we will refer to them again in other parts of the continent. The floor plan of pit houses is generally round, with four main uprights set in the ground in a square or rectangle to support the primary roof beams. The entry for people and exit for smoke is a hole in the center of the roof. A similar construction plan is followed in some Rio Grande Pueblos in kiva building.

This is not to suggest that the pit house is ancestral to all other American Indian dwellings, or that the cultures in which pit houses are found are related. It is only an observation that in all the variety of house types known to have been constructed and used by American Indians, pit houses were the most widely distributed in both time and space.

The unique feature of the Mimbres culture is its pottery. A hard-fired gray-white or buff ware was decorated with fine line drawings in black or dark red. Sometimes Mimbres decoration is geometric; sometimes it is representational of human, animal, or supernatural figures. It is characterized by humor, and sometimes by grotesquerie. Mimbres pottery is totally unlike any other ware, and so much of it has been found in a few ruins, occupied simultaneously, as to suggest that a family of potters is responsible for most of the production.

Like many other Indian groups, the Mimbres disappeared into obscurity before the Europeans entered the southwest.

The great achievement of the Hohokam was their engineering. Not only did they build the great ball courts and lay out the avenues of their ceremonial cities; they developed systems of canal irrigation, taking the floodwater from the rivers and spreading it out through series of secondary canals into their fields.

Although the Hohokam were still in the stage of horticulture where they worked with mesquite-root digging sticks and deer scapulae hoes, their irrigation systems were far beyond the stage their tools would indicate. On aerial photographs today the lines of the ditches still show, as straight and true as if surveyed with the most modern engineering equipment. The walls of the ditches were lined with sun-hardened clay to prevent as much seepage as possible. Control gates must have been installed, but we do not know how these were regulated.

Even before the Spaniards entered the area, Hohokam culture had passed its peak and had descended into a series of scattered horticultural communities, where the people laid great emphasis on funerary rites and observed few other formalized religious practices. It would hardly be an exaggeration to say that the first Spaniards simply walked through these people, hardly noticing them, for detailed written accounts do not begin until the eighteenth century, when missionary activities really began among the Hohokam descendants.

And what was there that the Spaniards would want in this howling desert? It might have occurred to them that the Cities of Cibola lay west, not east, of the Pueblo country, but apparently it did not. All that the explorers saw, among the ocotillo, cactus, mesquite, and creosote bushes that dotted the sand, was a series of huddled villages, scattered small cornfields, and people who toiled endlessly gathering wild plant foods and trapping small rodents on the uplands or tasteless fish in the muddy rivers.

Perhaps the acceptance of fish as a staple of diet by the river Yuman-speakers had a lost root in the Hohokam dependence on the rivers as a source of agricultural water, and is reflected in the many fish painted on Mimbres bowls. This is pure speculation. We do know that even into historic times these people alone in the southwest have accepted fish as an edible commodity, not something to be avoided and feared.

Where did the Hohokam proper go? Precisely what descendants did they leave behind them? How and by whom were they swallowed up? These are questions to which we do not yet know the answers. The People Who Went Before left evidence of their engineering skill, of their great gifts as craftsmen in shell, metal, turquoise, and pottery, and in the caves of the mesas and dry soils of the desert cities, of their skill as basket makers and as weavers, but that is all. It would be too much to say that the Hohokam vanished from the face of the earth. They simply fell apart.

Studies of Yuman, Mohave, Piman, and Papago mythologies in the twentieth century lead us to believe that for these peoples the end of life was its end. The body of a deceased person was cremated, with all that person's worldly goods. There seems to have been little concept or understanding of life hereafter, little centralization of government or of social organization, only an extreme individualism and independence of personalities.

Yet *somebody* organized the populations that built those cities and irrigation systems. Somebody was responsible for the expeditions that set out, probably annually, for the Gulf of California to bring back shells and salt, whether these items were gathered or obtained through trade. Somebody had the group concept of working together, in the middle twelfth and thirteenth centuries.

Were the Spaniards right, and was it from here that Moctezuma and his Aztec followers came, to organize all of Mexico and to conquer and weld its peoples into an empire? Perhaps, some day, we shall find out.

Not until 1687 did Father Kino come from California to establish missions among the desert peoples. They were then as they have been since, patient, adaptable to an inhospitable environment, gatherers and trappers and basket makers, who could listen to his preaching of a Christian god, accept it easily, and forget it quickly, for they had no strong and deeply rooted religious convictions of their own.

8

Storm Out of the North

PERHAPS BOTH HOHOKAM AND ANASAZI HAD BEEN VICtims of the epidemic we have postulated for the depopulation of the Mississippi Valley between A.D. 1000 and 1500. In the case of the Hohokam, it caused disaster and the wiping out of populations. In the case of the Anasazi it caused movements out of the high country of the Four Corners and into the open lands along the New Mexico rivers.

But the epidemic is only a postulate. A far more likely explanation for the shifts and changes of Indian populations is the storm which swept down on the southwest from the far northwest at about the same period: the Athabascan invasion.

In a sense the Athabascans, whom we know as the Apache and the Navaho, are a living link between the people of the Archaic period and those of today; between the simple hunting and gathering material cultures of the Great Basin and Plateau countries and the more complex horticultural populations of the southwest. The Athabascans came almost empty-handed, and now their hands are full.

In another sense, the southern Athabascans are cultural vacuum cleaners. They can, will, and do adopt any culture trait that seems to them desirable, and adapt it to their own purposes. Who today thinks of "Indian silverwork" as anything but Navaho? Yet the northeastern tribes were working in the imported metal as early as the seventeenth century, as we know from ethnohistorical sites that have been excavated, and the tribes of the Mississippi Valley and the Great Plains learned the craft in the late eighteenth century. Today "Indian" and "Navaho" are synonymous in connection with silver jewelry, although there are many skilled silversmiths working in other parts of the country.

In the same spirit, the Athabascans acquired everything else that caught their fancy. When they first came into the southwest, they were lurkers, armed with bows but equally at home with throwing spears, traps, and nets as a means of acquiring food. They probably were not particular about their diet, as compared with the Anasazi gourmets, for tribes of the Great Basin still eat lizards, land turtles, grasshoppers, and certain caterpillars when other foods are lacking.

The Athabascans took readily to cultivated foods when they encountered them. Gathering of wild grass seeds and other wild plants, fruits, nuts, and berries was laborious work, and it was easier to get vegetable foods by raiding the Anasazi gardens than by toiling over uplands and along valleys to pick up what there was to be found and eaten on the spot or carried home, probably in nets slung over the shoulders, or in baskets.

How far north the Athabascans were when they started southward nobody knows. Their name for themselves, Déné, is the same word that the Athabascan-speaking tribes of the Mackenzie River basin in Canada apply to their own group. Not that the two languages are mutually intelligible, except for a few words. But the southern Athabascans have retained a Déné word which means canoe, although they live in high, dry country where there are few navigable rivers and nobody ever used canoes. The northern Athabascans are fish eaters; the southerners regard fish as their ancestors and fish-eating with abhorrence, as an act of cannibalism.

The northern Déné lived, in historic times, in brush-thatched or skin-covered tipis, and a similar type of dwelling is to be found among their southern relatives. The southerners also had modified pit houses, somewhat similar in structure to Hohokam houses, or they plastered their dwellings with clay, a rude version of the Anasazi Pueblo building in puddled adobe. Later, when the railroads introduced timbers of uniform size, in the form of ties, the Navaho developed the *hogan* and made it peculiarly their own: an eight-sided wooden building, open to the east, with a cribbed roof like that of a pit house and a central smoke hole, but constructed on ground level. It is the hogan, its size and proportions dictated by the length of railroad ties, that one sees most often now on the Navaho reservation in Arizona and New Mexico.

It has been suggested by some writers that the Athabascans, north and south, represent the last wave of migration from Asia, and that they did not reach North America until a few hundred years before the Christian era. It may be so. Archaeolinguistics are being used in an effort to relate Déné to known western Asiatic languages.

From about A.D. 900 the Athabascans began to take over in the southwest—we do know that. They were in the area and were firmly rooted when the Spaniards arrived; in fact, the conquistadors encountered wildish groups to whom they gave the Zuni name for enemy—Apache—almost as soon as they encountered the Zuni.

At first, the Athabascans were more a nuisance to the Spaniards than a menace. The Apaches were slave owners, another far northern trait, and they raided the villages as much for captives as for wealth and food. From the Pueblo captives the Athabascans learned as they learned from everyone, and by the time of the Spanish occupation one group was known to them as *los Apaches del Nabajo* —the enemy people of the plowed fields.

The Navaho learned more than horticulture from their slaves. They learned weaving from the Pueblo men, who had great skill in this craft. The first fibers used were sotol or yucca threads, cotton, and the hair of specially bred dogs. In order to put their slaves in their place and keep them there, the Navaho required that the Anasazi men teach weaving to the Navaho women.

Many of the Apache groups were highly skilled basket makers, although the Navaho never seem to have excelled at this craft. They, like some other southern Athabascans, did develop a crude pottery, distinguished by its pointed bottom—made so the vessel could be set in the cooking fire—with simple rim decoration. It did not compare with the vividly decorated pottery of the Anasazi and Hohokam craftswomen, and probably was used only by the more settled Navaho groups. Pitch-coated basketry canteens and plain basket bowls were lighter and easier to carry around on foot.

Much of their religion and rituals the Athabascans developed from their Pueblo neighbors. The night-long dances, whose sequential pageantry consumes from four to eight nights, were performed in costumes similar to those worn by the Pueblo *kachinas*—dancers who represented the supernatural beings who are also known as kachinas.

But whereas in the villages the movements of the dancers are smooth and controlled, and their scattering of cornmeal gentle and restrained, the Navaho Yei-bi-chai and the Gahan, or mountain spirit dancers of the Apache, leaped and cavorted, and cast cornmeal about them with a lavish hand.

It is tempting to hazard a guess that in their northern homes the Athabascans had known considerable illness and much suffering, for their whole concept of religion became based on the *restoration* of health. The Anasazi must have assumed, as their descendants still do, that a whole person, a "real" person, is a well person, for few of their ceremonies are healing ones. The Athabascans apparently assume that sickness is a part of life, a dreaded reality but a reality, and that the gods must be invoked to restore, rather than to maintain, health.

With the fear of sickness went a panic fear of death. The dying were often carried out of their homes, for if death took place indoors the house and all its contents had to be burned. Even to use the wood from a hogan in which a death had occurred for a cooking fire at a far later date would invite the dread *chindi*—the spirit of the dead person—who would attack Indians and non-Indians without discrimination.

Owls were the harbingers of death, spirits who returned to the living to call one of them into the afterworld. Bears were almost as much feared as owls, for it was said that bears, like fish, were ancestral to men, and that bears could have sexual intercourse with human beings. The Athabascans walked through a world of terror, seeking to placate the beings who inhabited it with sung prayers whose repeated refrain is:

In beauty all things begin . . .
In beauty I walk . . .
In beauty it is finished.

It is as if the invocation of the beautiful—and good—spirits were a protection in itself.

No culture of the southwest was so deeply changed by the Spanish invasion as that of the Athabascans. They quickly learned to appropriate horses and burros from the conquerors or from the village peoples. They also learned to crossbreed these animals and obtain mules, which the western Apaches, particularly, considered superior to either parent for riding, packsaddle work, or food.

But the greatest discovery of Athabascan life was sheep and goats. These animals changed everything. They were a readily available source of food. They could be herded by women and children, ranging as far from the home camp as the shepherds could walk. Above all, sheep and the long-haired goats were a source of textile fibers. Skin clothing could be abandoned for garments made of cloth. Robes and dresses were simple affairs, for no North American Indian group acquired the skill of tailoring in cloth. Garments were always woven to the size to be worn.

Better yet, sheep, goats, wool, and textiles could be traded to the Spanish settlers or to the trading trains that were beginning to move north from Mexico. From being poor people, skulkers in the brush and eaters of rodents, the Athabascans knew prosperity by the eighteenth and early nineteenth centuries, for they were by nature shrewd traders and observant opportunists.

Everything could still be threatened and destroyed by the bad spirits and their servants, the witches. True, Pueblo peoples feared witchcraft, but they had good witches to whom they could turn for protection in the physical world. The Athabascans had their "curing doctors" of course, but Athabascan doctors set their fees high and did not go to work without an advance payment. The witches had a fertile field of the imagination in which to develop fear and to control their neighbors through a kind of spiritual blackmail, for if identified, they could be bought off.

These then were the people who descended on the Anasazi and changed Anasazi life as profoundly as the Spaniards changed Athabascan culture. Fierce, possessive, shrewd, demanding, and afraid, these people left their mark on the southwest as no others have; they are today the best businessmen and the shrewdest managers of all North American Indians. And these are the people who to many non-Indians are synonymous with the word "Indian" and the crafts of textiles and metalworking.

9

Along the Borders

BORDER PEOPLE EVERYWHERE SEEM TO BE MORE SUSCEPTIBLE to change than mountaineers or settled farmers. So it was with the peoples of the central United States, those who lived on the margins of the Great Plains at the time of the first European discoveries of the continent.

Our first records of these groups come, of course, from archaeologists who have excavated prehistoric and protohistoric villages along the drainages of the Upper Republican, the Dismal, the Platte, and other river tributaries of the Missouri, as well as along the upper reaches of the mainstream itself.

Reading field and site reports, one is driven to the conclusion that life was as dull for these peoples as it was adventurous for their historic descendants. The marginal Plains archaeological sites are characterized by pit houses: some larger, some smaller, with the usual tunnel entrances and circle-around-a-square floor plans. Fire pits and storage caches have been found in the pounded earth floors of these houses with remains of a small-cob type of corn, some beans and squash seeds, and many bones of small game.

Mixed with other animal remains are a few buffalo and deer bones, principally scapulae, which may have been used as hoes. Stone and bone awls are abundant, an indication that the women worked long and hard tailoring skin garments and stitching moccasins. A few textiles have been recovered, but only in tattered fragments. The indications here are that cloth was finger-woven, not loom-woven, and closely related to the fabrics of the Great Lakes and central Mississippi Valley.

Pottery was thick-walled and coiled, and had little decoration, but it was abundant. Here as nowhere else on the continent is the anthropological flippancy true that every sherd is a site and every site is a culture. Pottery occurs as frequently in the river-bottom sites as stone tools or implements or weapons. All these were plentiful.

Most of the stone points and tools were flaked, but a few heavier implements, like hammers, were ground. Stone mortars and pestles have been found, these also shaped by grinding, which leads us to believe that the women made meal from corn and wild seeds, and there was sufficient dependency on plant foods to require special utensils for their preparation.

There is evidence, especially in the northern Plains, that the people engaged in communal buffalo hunts. Plowing at the foot of some steep-sided bluffs has turned up piles of thousands of animal bones. The bones could only have accumulated in such quantities by driving the buffalo over the bluffs and butchering them where they fell.

The first European to visit the northern margin of the Plains was Pierre de la Vérendrye, who reached the Dakotas from New France in 1734, traveling principally by canoe and portage along the rivers. He naturally claimed the area for France and dutifully returned reports of the earth lodge villages and of the lives the people lived in them.

Vérendrye particularly commented on the communal buffalo hunts, and how the women went out with their skinning knives, butchered and skinned the great animals, and returned to camp with their meat lashed to poles that were dragged by dogs. The dogs and their burdens were especially interesting to Vérendrye. That animals so near wolves could be tamed, trained, and controlled was a small miracle to him. Dog breeding was often the task of women, and it was the women who managed the drag dogs outside the village.

Trapping was good along the lakeshores and beside the rivers, where otters, beavers, muskrats, and other fur-bearing animals abounded. But beyond the shores and their skirting woodlands extended the vast inland sea of the Great Plains, and the Frenchman could see nothing there worth traveling for. Like the eastern Indians, the French, as we have said, were waterborne, and they were not greatly interested in country where they could not travel by canoe.

That vast, rolling country, cut through by shallow seasonal streams, with only a few rivers that ran all the year around, would have daunted anybody. Grass grew high in the lowlands, low on the upper crests of the land waves; and to a vision that was accustomed to hills and valleys, the Plains looked desolately flat and empty. Only the buffalo herds waded through its spaciousness, and it seemed that only animals huge as buffalo—least of all puny men—could face its endlessness.

But there were animals who would conquer the space of the Plains and the buffalo as well: horses, burros, and mules. Before De Vargas' *reentrada* the first escaped animals fell into Indian hands. Probably the route of diffusion of horses was from Oñate's capital at San Juan, through trade and theft via the other northern Pueblos, especially Taos, and so into the hands of the southern Plains people: Comanche, Kiowa, and Kiowa-Apache. It could not have begun much earlier than the Pueblo rebellion, for Oñate had been the first of the Spaniards to bring breeding stock, and the Pueblo uprising undoubtedly set horses loose that would otherwise have been corralled and picketed.

The Spaniards had learned their horse culture from the Moors of northern Africa; it is one of the many traits which make Renaissance Spanish culture distinct from the cultures of northern Europe. Not only the horses and donkeys themselves, but saddles, bridles, headstalls, reins, trappings, stirrups, and ornaments were of Moorish derivation. The Spaniards took them over lock, stock, and barrel.

With horses and their equipment went a set of mental and emotional attitudes that were almost indistinguishable from the beasts. Moorish and Spanish horses were not bred to pull plows or carts. They were bred for racing and fighting, to carry mounted men in battle or elegant ladies mounted on padded sidesaddles in hunting. The very word for "gentleman" derived from the name of the horse, *caballo;* one of high birth was a *caballero*—a mounted man.

Priests of all degrees rode donkeys or mules, as tokens of humility and obedience to the dictates of Jesus. In the case of cardinals, archbishops, and other nobles of the Church, who were themselves of noble birth and blood, these animals were as fine and as highly bred as saddle horses, and their equipment hardly suggested humility.

This emotional complex, and the equipment for the horses, spread with the animals. Horses became the be-all and the end-all of the Indians who lived on the margins of the Plains. Like the Pueblo and southern Athabascan Indians, those of the southern Plains copied, in wood and antler and rawhide, the metal saddles and trappings of the Spaniards.

Horses, tack, and emotional values spread northward rapidly, probably by way of the Comanche to their relatives, the Shoshoni, and from there to other tribes. It was like a fire sweeping through the Plains grasses. "A man afoot was no man at all," then or later.

A man on horseback ruled the world. He could ride out onto the sea of grass and bring down the buffalo, one at a time or many in succession, as he needed them. Bows were shortened and spears were lengthened for greater mobility and efficiency. As mounted tribe encountered mounted tribe, a new language had to be invented. Otherwise speakers of different languages could not have communicated their peaceful or warlike intentions to one another. Sign language, or hand talk, soon developed.

Dr. Ruth Underhill has referred to "The Newly Rich People of the Plains," and the phrase certainly seems applicable. As the men swept out in pursuit of the buffalo, and hides accumulated, the women found an ever increasing number of uses for leather. It could be used to cover the poles that formerly were thatched with brush or covered with sheets of bark. The tipi, probably the most efficient shelter possible for a migrant people, was invented.

Now that there were horses to drag the shelter poles, the poles were longer and the shelters larger. Dogs were still bred and kept; one drag horse replaced four dogs, as a rule, but the dogs were indispensable for small objects. Usually the drag horses were mares or geldings. Another trait of Moorish derivation was keeping down the size of the herds and improving the stock by castrating surplus stallions. The drag horses usually belonged to the women who used them; Plains Indian men were more interested in fast, surefooted mounts for hunting and fighting.

By the middle of the 1700's, Plains Indian culture was completely mobile. Pottery making was a forgotten art and basket making almost gone; rawhide containers were lighter and easier to carry about than earthen vessels. The textile skills had been abandoned; soft-tanned skin clothing was easier to make, warmer in winter and cooler in summer. Two-piece moccasins with hard rawhide soles replaced the soft-soled one-piece footgear of the woodland tribes.

What we often think of as "the typical Indian culture" reached its peak about 1800. Altogether, it lasted only a little more than a hundred years. But in that short time, Plains Indian culture left its mark on the whole world. It became symbolic of freedom, of the footloose, fancy-free, unfenced existence that all men everywhere must dream of at some time in their lives. To Euro-Americans who first encountered Plains culture, it was a dazzling thing, much more exciting than life lived in mud-walled villages and tied to the whims of water and the seasons.

Plains Indian culture, outwardly, was a man's world. A man's achievements were marked by the number of enemies he touched bare-handed or with a short stick in battle rather than by those he killed. He might take the scalp of a dead or dying enemy—few people survived the treatment—home to show his women, but it was far braver to strike a living foe than to scalp a dead one.

Achievement also was counted in terms of the number of horses or women obtained, by night and by stealth, from other tribes. As stock and breeding improved, the range of the raids extended, until no village in northern Mexico had not given up its share of captives, and such a thing as a "pure" strain of blood did not exist in any Plains tribe, so intermarried with captives or with the children of friends did their members become.

At the same time, the men had their periods of celibacy. As their woodland ancestors had done, Plains Indian men sought the protection and counsel of spirit guardians by fasting alone in secluded places. During these vision quests the men neither ate nor drank, but smoked, sang, and prayed.

The spirit guardian might take the form of a plant or animal; of a cloud formation; of a particular voice crying along the wind. Perhaps a blood offering was made to invoke a spirit; a man gashed his arms, legs, and breast with his knife, cut off his hair, or even sacrificed a finger joint in order that he might "dream true."

During and after the vision quest the man observed continence, and often required it of all the members of his family. Other taboos might be imposed by the spirit, such as abstinence from certain foods or water from a particular stream, the wearing of a certain color or sitting in a particular place or position. A token of the guardianship was sometimes given; the visionary was commanded to wear an eagle claw or a stone arrowpoint as a talisman, perhaps. Sometimes the dreamer might reveal his dream; at other times he was bidden to lock it in the secret places of his heart.

There were no priests, as such. Each man was his own priest. Even the men who guarded such tribal tokens as the Sacred Arrows of the Cheyenne, the Flat Pipe of the Arapaho, or the Sun Dance figure—the Taime—of the Kiowa did so as individuals, and as individuals they trained their successors to guardianship. Group action was possible in any Plains tribe, but between the times when it was necessary, rugged individualism prevailed.

Certain ceremonies, like the midsummer Sun Dance, required the presence of the whole tribal population. Not until the four days of preparation and the four days of dancing against the sun with the accompanying fasting, blood offerings, prayers, and songs of suffering were over, were men supposed to set out on war parties or to organize communal hunts.

A Sun Dance encampment, with all the tribe gathered, together with visitors from other tribes, white traders after the whites had discovered this fertile field of trade, and wandering strangers of any kind, might include as many as 5,000 people. At this one time the tipis were not set facing eastward in irregular streets but were formed into a great circle, with each door facing inward, toward the Sun Dance lodge and its ceremonies.

To keep order in such camps, and also in the great hunts, men's societies were organized. On such occasions the members of one or more societies, as the Sun Dance chief might designate, were police, game wardens, and fire watchers simultaneously. A fire that broke out in one tipi could spread rapidly through the whole camp, leaving panic and destruction in its wake.

Criers went through camp at regular intervals, calling out the names of the bands: "South People! Biters! Prairie People! Visitors! Women, put out your fires. When you leave your tipis, cover the fires with ashes. Look out for the little ones, and see that they are safe! All you people, obey the Dog Soldiers who tell you these things!" And the Dog Soldiers were obeyed, or as the Cheyenne put it, the disobedient ones were "soldiered"; their goods destroyed and scattered and their faces shamed.

So much can be and has been written about the Plains culture that it is easy to lose the forest of thought in the trees of detail. It is as easy to overromanticize here as it is in writing about the Rio Grande villagers. There was stir and excitement in a Plains Indian camp, truly. There still is, during a midsummer powwow. So much so that it was easy to forget the scolding women, the yapping, snapping dogs, the flies, the babies who undoubtedly needed changing, and the stampeding horse herds that might sweep across the prairie.

It is easy to forget or romanticize or draw a veil over the torture of prisoners, the keeping of slaves until everyone but the slaves themselves forgot they were not tribal-born, and the destruction of property when a family mourned a death.

Far pleasanter to think of a united family—a man, his first wife, and her sisters or cousins whom he had subsequently married, with children who were surer who their father was than who their mother was—gathered about the tipi fire for a winter evening of feasting and storytelling, than to think of the winter evenings when there was no food to feast on and families lived on "tight belts and water."

Plains culture was remarkably homogeneous, because of the rapidity of its spread and the brevity of its duration. It came out of holes in the ground, spread like a grass fire across the heart of a continent, and died to ashes under railroad wheels. Yet, while it lasted, the Plains culture was a mighty thing.

Tell their names over, for they are not gone yet: Comanche, Kiowa, Apache, Cheyenne, Arapaho, Blackfoot, the mighty and magnificent Sioux, Arikara, Mandan, Hidatsa, Crow, and Pawnee—there will not be a name on the list that is unfamiliar to the average literate European or American. Latecomers, new rich, exploiters of weaker peoples—the Plains tribes were all these things. But they have survived, and their later stories, too, will be told in this book.

10

Poverty-Poor

THE SLASH-AND-BURN, HIT-AND-RUN TACTICS OF THE Plains Indians in warfare, wife-stealing, and hunting demanded small, light horses, quick on their feet and of considerable endurance. Most of them seem to have been about the size and general conformation of today's quarter horses. Many resembled the original Barbary breed and were known by Spanish words. The preferred colors were blue (known usually as *grullo*), buckskins with white manes and tails (palominos), and buckskins with dark points and a dark streak down the middle of the back (*bayos coyotes*, or coyote bays). Painted (pinto) horses, or those that were dappled, were considered unreliable in temper and lacking in endurance. The Plains Indians preferred to have nothing to do with such beasts.

It remained for the Nez Perce, on the northwest margin of the Plains, to develop the only true American-bred horse, the Appaloosa. These horses were strongly marked, with a dark bay or sorrel background color and white splotches making a saddle on the back and sides. Often they were distinguished by white pigmentation on the face or head, an unacceptable marking by Moorish, Spanish, or Plains standards. Appaloosas were and are large horses, heavier and stronger than quarter horses and capable of carrying heavier loads.

There may have been a strain of English thoroughbred blood in the original Appaloosas, for the Nez Perce lived on either side of the border, and English traders were beginning to find their way westward overland. By the time the true Appaloosas, as distinguished from haphazard painted (or pinto) horses were developed, the English controlled Canada.

But before the introduction of horses, the tribes on the western margins of the Plains, in the Great Basin and Plateau areas between the Rockies and the Sierras, were to the outer eye a pitiful huddle of starving souls. Their material culture was relatively simple; small, single-family pit houses, with larger semisubterranean communal dance houses for ceremonies, or racked-up poles covered with brush and grass for hunting parties, were their only shelters.

There was large game in the northern part of this area, but finding it and hunting it down was toilsome work. The Plateau-Basin peoples developed an unusually effective hunting bow, for they hunted on foot and could not afford to waste arrows. These compound bows were made of hardwood, usually mountain mahogany, and were bent in a double curve, with the inward central bend coming at the grasp of the archer's hand, and the two outward curves jutting at the ends where the bowstring was secured.

These bows were shaped by steaming and heating over hot wood or water or low fires. When the desired shape had been reached, the bowstave received further finishing and forming by being scraped with a piece of obsidian, or volcanic glass, until the wood itself was glassy smooth. After that, layer on layer of deer sinew—the heavy muscle that overlies the tenderloin on the back of a grazing animal—was applied to the inner surface of the stave. If sinew is dampened, it becomes gluey and will adhere to wood, to hide, or to itself. When the sinew dries it dries iron hard, and a bow so strengthened is practically unbreakable and shoots with terrific force. Although these compound bows are short, and look most unimposing by comparison with the six-foot staves used by the eastern tribes, they are as effective as the European crossbows and have a longer range than any simple, unbacked wooden bow.

The arrows used with these weapons were also short, and were fletched with hawk feathers or with the feathers of water birds. Three vanes, twined around the arrow shaft, were the usual number of feathers, in distinction from the straight fletching with two or four feathers that was common in the Plains and among the eastern tribes. Bows and arrows, in fact, greatly resembled the weapons of some Mongolian tribes, and have been used as an argument for the late migration of Basin-Plateau peoples.

Even more usual hunting weapons in this area, though, were the nets and clubs used on communal rabbit hunts. Some of the nets, which were made by knotting twisted yucca-fiber cords, were as much as 500 feet long and 10 feet wide. With such a net a large area could be surrounded; the rabbits were driven into its center by men, women, boys, and girls and there clubbed to death. The meat was dried and stored for winter use.

Wild plant seeds, grasses, and the roots of camas and water lilies formed the staples of Basin-Plateau diets. From early spring until snow fell, each season had a plant or plants to be gathered, and women and children toiled endlessly with short digging sticks and great harvest baskets to gather food to bring home and store in pit caches.

People wore little clothing. In summer women wore aprons of shredded cedar bark, tied around their waists, with perhaps necklaces of seeds or partly ground shells. Men wore buckskin breechclouts. In winter the members of both sexes exchanged their summer sandals of twined rushes for elk-skin or sometimes buffalo-hide moccasins, made with the hair turned in for added warmth.

And in winter, both sexes wore blankets of twined rabbit-skin cloth. From the Archaic period on, this cloth had such a wide distribution in both time and space that it deserves special mention. Anasazi and Hohokam alike made and wore it. The Hopi made it. The Athabascans made it. Scraps have been found in cave sites from Nevada to Arkansas and back again by way of the Big Bend of Texas and the Sierra Madre of northern Mexico. It was known in preconquest times and later along the Columbia River as well as along the Rio Grande. Rabbit-fur cloth was almost ubiquitous in the Archaic period, and it continued to be made at least until 1969.

The weaver began, of course, by preparing the strands from which the fabric was to be twined. Beginning at the outer edge of the rabbit skin, originally with a knife of obsidian or some other sharp stone, a strip of rabbit skin was cut, around and around, until the center of the skin was reached. The whole skin was rolled into a ball as big around as a tennis ball—or sometimes larger—and set aside while other skins were cut in the same manner. When enough balls of skin, each one a continuous strip of rabbit hide, had been accumulated, the worker proceeded to the next step.

This was to twist the rabbit fur strand with one of plant fiber: yucca, wild nettle, cedar or cedar-root bark—whatever was available. A strand of each fiber was laid on the worker's bare thigh and rolled between the thigh and the palm of the hand. Care was taken to have the core of the strand of plant fiber, the outer surface of rabbit skin. The job sounds endless, but in reality a skilled worker could accumulate a large ball of combined-fiber cordage in a day.

Then came the actual twining. Pegs were set in the ground to make a square or rectangle of the desired size. A continuous selvage thread was stretched around them. Back and forth, from the upper to the lower selvage as the garment would be worn, ran the warps, the strong supporting threads that are the basis of every fabric. These, again, were made of plant fibers. And then, working with two strands of fur-covered yarn, the worker moved across the warps from edge to edge. At each intersection the two weft strands changed places; the one below was brought to the upper surface of the blanket. As the strands passed each other, each was firmly twisted, or twined, around the warp strand.

This, like the finger weaving of the east, produced a large and usable piece of cloth. The fleas that were native to the rabbits, and embedded in the fur after their hosts had died, were handily disposed of by letting the blanket lie out on the ground or hang suspended from a line in freezing weather.

Twining also characterized much of the basketry of the Basin-Plateau country, although some coiled, or sewn, baskets were also made. Here the aesthetic expression of a simple material culture reached a peak seldom equaled elsewhere. Designs and execution alike were of the finest quality.

Baskets were used for everything by the Plateau peoples. Seeds were parched by shaking them on a basket tray with live coals. Mush and meat stews were boiled by dropping hot stones into watertight baskets. Bowls and cups were basketry. Basket beaters were used to gather wild seeds; babies' cradles were made of nets or baskets. Gathering baskets held several bushels of seeds at a time and were carried by tumplines, plaited or twined cloth bands passed across the bearers' foreheads and resting against basket pads or basket hats.

Willow, dogwood, cedar, rushes, cattails, mountain mahogany bark, yucca, sotol—any fiber-yielding plant that grew on the desert uplands or along the shallow streams or the banks of the muddy lakes furnished the Basin-Plateau people with a source of basket material. The preparation of fibers was a constant preoccupation of the women in summer: plaiting, twining, and sewing baskets were their winter jobs.

As if to compensate for the rugged environment and simple material life they led, the Basin-Plateau peoples developed an elaborate system of ceremonials. The "rites of passage," or the observances of physical changes and transitions of individuals, were highly developed. There were puberty rites for both boys and girls; there were menstrual and childbirth taboos which isolated women at such periods. Here alone in North America the couvade, the custom by which a father is isolated and cared for when his wife gives birth, has been reported. The couvade is best known to Europeans among the Basques of northern Spain, but it was an old and highly developed custom among the Ute, the Paiute, the Washo, and their neighbors long before Basque sheepherders ever saw the Utah, Nevada, and Idaho uplands.

Here the people lived their relatively uncomplicated lives well into the nineteenth century. They held their elaborate funerals and cremations. They avoided bears and owls, for the same reason that other tribes to the south and east of them did; they hunted and went gathering wherever plants grew, and they got along. To European eyes they had nothing and they were nothing. "Diggers," the first Europeans called them, watching the women turn up roots and fat white grubs and eat both indiscriminately. When they observed that grasshopper legs and the crushed scorched bodies of certain caterpillars were also a part of the family menu, the Europeans hurried on and left these savages to their own devices.

The devices included not only the rituals we have mentioned but a complex kinship system, a highly developed vision quest, the curing of illness by specially trained doctors, and a high standard of oratory and poetry. These are not culture traits that leap to foreign eyes, and so the seekers for gold and furs may be forgiven for hurrying by with no record of what they regarded as the disgusting habits of a primitive people.

These were not primitive people; they were highly sophisticated. They had heard tales and seen the survivors of smallpox epidemics, of cholera outbreaks, of wanton massacres. The Basin-Plateau people liked their life the way it was and hoped to keep on living it that way. And nobody had ever heard of uranium.

11

California Unchanging

THERE WERE PASSES ACROSS THE SIERRAS AND THE CAScades, and people and ideas went back and forth from the coast to the inland regions.

In a way, California then, as now, was a stopping-off place, a halfway house between the Basin-Plateau area and the intricate culture of the northwest coast. Reports of the California coast returned to England in 1580, when Sir Francis Drake reported on his voyage around the globe begun in 1577.

Drake landed in the vicinity of San Francisco Bay and remained on the coast, for "Drake he was a Devon man. And he sailed the Devon seas," and even London, by all accounts, was a long way inland for him. He claimed the seemingly endless curving coastline for Queen Elizabeth and England, and departed with no comment except that seals were abundant among the rocks.

Even before Drake's landfall and claim, in 1542, Juan Rodríguez Cabrillo had landed farther south on the California coast and reported fertile inland valleys and good grazing lands. He had claimed southern California for Spain, but nothing was done about colonizing the area until after the settlement of New Mexico and Arizona.

The connection between the fertile southern California valleys and the seal rocks of the northern coast was no clearer than the relation of either area to the southwest. England claimed all the land from the Atlantic westward, with specific additional claim to the Bay area; Spain claimed all the land from the vicinity of San Diego eastward, and where these claims overlapped was anybody's guess. The only sure thing was that the claims conflicted somewhere.

In 1769 Father Junípero Serra began systematically establishing missions in southern California, so successfully that the native population became known as Mission Indians. The chain of missions stretched northward from San Diego to the Mission Dolores, at San Francisco. Many of these missions are still standing; some are in ruins, and some have been restored. They are monuments not only to the fervor of the eighteenth-century Franciscans but to the amount of work the Spaniards were able to extract from subject peoples.

Here, along the mission chain, the living was easy for anybody but white men in the preconquest period. The California Indians wore little clothing, went barefoot, and lived in pit houses or brush shelters. They relied principally on fishing and gathering for their food. The real staple of diet was the acorns of the great oak trees of the area, which the Indians learned to roast, pound, and leach to extract the tannic acid. The resulting meal was reground, often in mortar holes pecked into standing boulders, and could be eaten as it was or cooked into mush by stone-boiling in baskets.

One fascinating source of speculation is the similarities between native populations in the United States and those which overwhelmed them. A caste system developed in the southeast, for instance, among the native Indians and among the white plantation owners. New Englanders of education and philosophic turn of mind are almost ineluctably drawn to the Hopi and other Pueblo peoples, their own Indians having been largely eliminated. And in California, both aboriginal and white population groups have laid great stress on minimal clothing and the acquisition and display of wealth.

The California Indians counted wealth in the form of great translucent blades, chipped from fragile obsidian and far too delicate to be of any use to anybody. They ground and strung dentalium shells, with so many inches of beads equaling the value of an obsidian blade. In order that there should be no mistake in measuring, men and women alike tatooed their forearms with gauges against which the strings of beads could be laid.

Above all, certain tribes excelled in the making of feather-covered baskets. The Pomo, in particular, specialized in this skill. The baskets were coiled, a willow-rod base being stitched with yucca or beach grass, and the feathers sewn into the stitches in the process. Pomo feather baskets are as large as mixing bowls and range downward to baskets the size of a pinhead. How feathers small enough to decorate these last were ever found, let alone worked with, is a miracle of the keen eyesight of the makers. Yet there the baskets are, complete even to tiny, recognizable designs, and perhaps with miniature dentalium shell beads stitched to their edges.

It is the absolute lack of utility in many of the Californian tokens of wealth that is startling. In the Plains, horses were the gauge of value. On the east coast it was fields and stores of corn, and the same was true in the southwest. But four-foot-long obsidian blades which broke if you looked at them, feathered baskets which could hardly be breathed on, and plain white dentalium shell beads, hard to grind and harder to preserve, are as useless as the albino deer skins which were the main fetishes in ceremonies.

Kinship systems were intricate. Households were simple, one-family units, usually clustered in villages. There was a considerable development of mythology and poetry, most of it now, unfortunately, lost. Tribes, clans, and bands interlocked, and clan relatives in other villages were known and avoided, for marriage was exogamous.

One of the great books on the American Indians, *Ishi*, by Theodora Kroeber, describes the life of the last survivor of the Yahi, one of the tribes of the Mount Lassen foothills area. It is a book that must be read to be believed. Ishi, the last of his people, managed to hide in the hills until he was a man in his fifties, when starvation finally forced him to seek the mercy of the white men. As luck would have it, Dr. Alfred Kroeber was then head of the Museum of Anthropology at San Francisco. He and Professor T. T. Waterman, also of the museum staff, went to Oroville, where Ishi had surrendered, and brought this living specimen of Stone Age man back to the museum.

It would not be fair to readers to tell the story here and now; Mrs. Kroeber has told it beautifully and touchingly, as the story of a dear friend, almost a member of the family. *Ishi* is a book that anyone can read and everyone should if he wishes to gain an insight into the life of California Indians.

It was a simple life; it could be lived with no more than hand tools and fire, if necessary. A sack of obsidian chips did for polishing and scraping. A pointed antler tip was used for flaking stone. The stone to be flaked was held in the palm of the hand, resting on the buckskin pad, and the antler tip was pressed against it. The pressure removed flakes, one at a time, and the finished arrow or spear point was ready in about an hour.

Women cut or plucked their hair and used the strands to twist into strings and work into nets for snares. Similar trip lines, fishing lines, and netted snares were made from bark fiber cordage. Baskets were twined or coiled from spruce or cedar bark. The cores of spruce or yew branches, painstakingly shaped and adjusted over steaming water and backed with sinew, made the short compound bows used for hunting or fighting.

Materially simple though the life of the California Indians was, it brought satisfaction to the people who lived it. At no time in native North America did men and women feel themselves "deprived" or "underprivileged." Men and nature were in balance; the resources of the environment were developed as they were explored and were allowed to continue to develop from year to year.

To read the story of Ishi is to read the story of a man who truly was born free, who protected himself and his family but did not harm anyone of his own volition, and who was finally "captured" because the balance of man and nature had been so disturbed that he could no longer maintain himself.

Ishi was not his name, for the word *ishi* means simply "man." No one ever knew what his name was, for it is a peculiarity of California tribes not to tell personal names. An individual had several names in his lifetime: a baby name, given at birth; a man's name, given in the course of an elaborate puberty ritual; perhaps three or four others taken to avoid evil spirits or misfortunes. But beyond all these was his *real* name, sometimes known only to the old person who had given it to him, and never to be spoken. It was not uncommon for an individual not to know what his real name was.

Instead of addressing one another by name, California Indians used age grade or relationship terms in conversation. If the person addressed was a stranger, a title of respect would be used to speak to him formally. He in turn would reply with a respect word, until he knew exactly the status of the greeter in his own group. The greatest curse was to speak aloud any one of the names of a deceased relative.

Whether one culture or another is intrinsically superior

is not, of course, a question that an anthropologist can decide, or even debate. Whether the advantages of the wheel, writing, metal tools and implements, and a superior technology outweigh the disadvantages of introduced diseases, changed food habits, obliterated populations, crafts, and kinship systems is not the point at issue in this book.

The only aim of a volume of ethnohistory is to state what went before, what encountered it, and what eventually emerged from the meeting. If we can even indicate the magnitude of change that took place in four hundred years, we shall have accomplished as much as we can.

So when we say that a culture was materially simple, we ask the reader to bear in mind that material simplicity can, and often does, as in California, go hand in hand with complexity of social structure and use of the environment to the fullest degree, along with poetry and music. We are not condemning—not even commenting, if we can help it—in most of this book. It is enough for us if we can tell something of what happened.

12

The Lumber Barons of the Northwest

THERE IS A CERTAIN SPECIFIC FIELD OF RESEARCH THAT is known as salvage archaeology. Crews of archaeologists move into an area where a dam or highway is projected, ahead of the construction crews. They first map possible archaeological sites. Then, following the bulldozers, the archaeologists watch to see what, if anything, the heavy machinery will turn up. If possible, the scientists then deflect the engineers and their employees to another scene of action and, working as quickly as they can, get out as much material as possible by hand labor, with pick and shovel.

In a sense, of course, all archaeology is salvage work. Archaeologists run an endless race against wind, weather, time, and the hands of other men. But salvage archaeology as such really began with the exploration of the Columbia River and its tributaries before the construction of the Grand Coulee Dam. It has continued to be a major preoccupation of archaeologists working in the northern river basins, and it is on their site reports that we must rely for information on the whole enormous stretch of Washington, British Columbia, the northwest coast as far as the Aleutians, and inland Canada as far east as the Hudson Bay area.

Perhaps we are writing this and the following chapter in reverse order. Archaeologists generally agree that the northern cultures began inland and descended the rivers to the Pacific. The coastal culture of the northwest, they tell us, is of more recent date than that of the vast inland area, although it is older than the classic culture of the Plains.

The coastal culture was the first to be encountered by Europeans, and the first to be recorded and described with any detail by them, and for that reason we shall describe it first. Formal claim on the coastline began with Captain James Cook's voyage of discovery in 1778, when he claimed British Columbia for England.

Even before Cook's voyage, the Russian whalers and sealers had worked the waters off the Alaskan shore, and in 1821 Czar Alexander I claimed the coastline of North America as far south as the 51st parallel of latitude for Russia.

Alexander's claim would eventually result in a complicated international political situation, but at the time it had no more than nuisance value. Everybody, including New Englanders from the new United States, who could get a ship into north Pacific waters took whales and seals as freely as everybody else, on or off shore. Russian records, if there were any official ones made, have so far remained unavailable to scientists in non-Communist countries, with a few exceptions.

The coming of the whalers and the sealers, and of the traders who inevitably followed them, had a profound effect on Northwest Coast Indian life. The introduction of metal tools brought about an efflorescence in their culture as pronounced as the development of Plains culture after the introduction of horses.

Probably the coastal people had always been workers in wood, but wood, in the humid climate of the north Pacific coast, is not an enduring substance. We will never know the exact extent of carving in wood that was done with stone tools. It must have been prolific, for it developed a unique art style.

The art style of the Northwest Coast Indians is remarkably homogenous from tribe to tribe. Tribal distinctions can and must be made by experts, of course. Overall, a distinguishing feature of Northwest Coast art is an abhorrence of vacant space. As nearly as possible, every inch of a given surface had to be filled.

This design concept features life forms, either anthropomorphic or zoomorphic. Many of the carvings represent the outward appearance of supernatural beings. In general, the figures are drawn to show each side, as if the creature depicted had been flattened out and then represented in cross section. In each joint appear small faces, and each joint must be shown. The Northwest Coast peoples were remarkably well-informed anatomists.

Representational art of this type, in low relief carving, appeared on house fronts, boxes, furniture, canoes, and the great records of family trees known as totem poles. Other totem poles were in full round carving, as were masks, rattles, weapons, and tools. What it must have cost in time, effort, and memory to carry the designs in mind from the first blow of the stone chisel to the last staggers the imagination.

This distinctive art style has parallels in two places: western China and some parts of Mexico. There is a steady effort on the part of art historians to link the three areas. It may yet be accomplished.

One particularly striking characteristic of some prehistoric and protohistoric carvings in the round is the appearance of the vertebrae on the surface of a figure. The bones are often correctly counted and depicted in position, although sometimes the size or shape of the stone that was being carved required simplification and the elimination of a few bones. One wonders if dampness-induced arthritis might have influenced the carvers' art.

Linguistically, there may be demonstrable links between the Northwest Coast peoples and those of the Asiatic mainland, as there are among the Eskimo. Archaeolinguists are still tussling with this problem. Now we can only say, with safety, that the Northwest Coast is unique and alone in its languages and in a single art style in North America.

The early explorers of southern Alaska, Vancouver Island, and British Columbia found the Indians living in great communal houses of split planks, with dormer roofs that were also covered with planks. The roof planks could be poked aside from within the long poles, to provide ventilation and chimneys. There were no nails, of course, so every part of the building was bound in place with cedar-root bark or juniper bark. Cedar, juniper, redwood, and white or yellow pine furnished the building materials.

Inside, the house was divided into beds, or one-family apartments, each screened from the other occupants of the building with sliding doors or hanging mats. In front of each enclosed bed was the family's fire for cooking and heating. Three or four stones, usually granite, were laid on the packed earthen floor to make a hearth.

In the center of the main building was the community fire, where meals were cooked jointly by the women of the several nuclear families when they wished to share the work. Here the extended family assembled for conferences, to receive visitors, for ceremonies, and for storytelling.

In the northwest generally, descent was reckoned through the father, and the men owned the houses. The extended or great household, then, consisted of a man, his wife or wives, and their sons and the sons' families. The patriarch occupied the place of honor, at the back of the building, facing the door. Young men, grown but still single, slept on either side of the doorway as guards.

"Patriarch" is a carefully chosen word, for among the Northwest Coast Indians there was an aristocracy intertwined with wealth unlike any other North American Indian culture area's social structure. Families were subdivisions of clans, and clans of tribes. Each tribe, clan, and individual held an assigned place dictated by inheritance through the male line.

In families in which male heirs were lacking, a daughter might be designated by her father to hold a social position and the name that went with it. In that case, the distinctions passed to her sons, and so out of the original family line.

Wealth was reckoned in terms of blankets woven from mountain sheep or dog hair. The actual making of the blankets was women's work, but the designs to be produced were heraldic in character and were drawn on boards by the men of the family, to be reproduced by the women. Women created geometric designs in the mats and baskets they twined for their own use. This type of design division was usual throughout North America.

So many woolen blankets equaled one copper. A "copper" is a shield-shaped piece of thinly beaten metal, sometimes three or four feet high, embossed with heraldic designs showing the descent of its original owner. A copper might pass through many hands, its value increasing with each interchange, until it reached its ultimate destruction or a resting place of honor in a museum. Coppers were made by special, highly skilled craftsmen.

The giving away of blankets and coppers was the occasion for a potlatch. At this time, a man summoned his friends and enemies, in order of rank, feasted them, and then bestowed coppers or blankets on those he wished to honor or to shame—again in order of rank. The most highly honored guests received the largest number of blankets and the most famous coppers. As blankets and coppers passed from hand to hand, in potlatch after potlatch, some of them became so famous that they were given names of their own.

If the host wished to insult an enemy, and bring him to the ultimate shame, he presented his foe with a broken copper or a torn blanket. Then it was economic war to the death, potlatch after potlatch, between the tribes, clans, and families involved.

Rank, established and supported by wealth, was everywhere. The size of the house, the number of persons feasted at one time, the position of each guest around the great carved wooden food bowl, the "totem" pole which depicted the history of a man's family and was erected before his house or above his grave so that all might see the greatness of his ancestors—all these were tokens of rank, inherited or purchased. For it was possible to purchase a vacant title, if the women of one family were industrious in twining and enough blankets and coppers could be accumulated through trade or outright purchase.

The potlatch has often been compared to the "give away" practiced by the Plains tribes, and both have been referred to as forms of aboriginal social security. In a sense the term is valid in the Plains, for there, if a person was known for his generosity in youth, he could expect care in return—in the form of gifts—in his old age. But a far more apt parallel in our society than social security would be conspicuous consumption: the kind of lavishness that celebrates a party for beautiful people in an expensive hotel, within a mile of some of the worst urban ghettos in the world. In such cases only the donors benefit, and that immediately, through the public bestowal of wealth or its tokens.

Another means of rigid social control besides the potlatch was shamanism. "Shaman" and its associated derivatives are of Asiatic origin, not only the word, but the function to which it refers. Shamanism is the causing of disease by the magical projection of a foreign body into the physical body of an enemy, and curing of the resulting illness by sucking to extract the object, which can then be destroyed. A shaman is one who practices this magical art, positively or negatively.

As with witches, there are good and bad shamans. Some have been known to use their power first to injure, then to obtain material rewards for the removal of the disease-causing object. At its extreme, this can become a form of blackmail; if the shaman does not get what he wants the first time of asking, he can cause the person who has offended him to become sick, then claim the desired object as a reward for curing him.

At the other end of the scale are shamans who *only* cure and treat disease rather than cause it. These are men usually well up in years, who are willing and able to dedicate themselves by a sort of Hippocratic oath to the well-being of others.

Notable stories have been told about battles between good and evil shamans, who can be readily distinguished from each other in the same manner as good and evil witches; the families of good shamans thrive, while those of wicked shamans rapidly decline in health and in number. If it is possible to determine which evil shaman has caused a certain illness, and to get to a good one in time, the death of the evildoer may result. There will be no ill effects in the life of his destroyer, for he has only eliminated what was already bad.

Shamanism is by no means confined to the Northwest Coast peoples. It is everywhere in Indian North America, possibly distributed by those culture go-betweens the Athabascans, who have developed it to considerable proportions. Shamanism does, however, reach a peak in the Northwest Coast area. There were whole societies of shamans, who held public and private ceremonies quite distinct from religious ceremonies.

The guardian spirit who assisted a shaman came unsought in many cases, and might give such tokens as material objects; the wearing of or abstaining from certain colors; and specific food taboos. Among the finest carvings and most beautiful specimens of Northwest Coast art are shamans' paraphernalia: rattles, spirit drums, charms to be used as X rays to discover the seat and the cause of an illness or to apply to the patient as tubes through which the disease-causing object could be sucked to the surface and extracted. The abundance of these objects in museums is testimony enough to the prevalence of shamanism on the Northwest Coast.

Wood was everywhere on the Northwest Coast. The war canoes, of riven planks, heated and bent into shape over boiling water, bound with cedar-bark rope and calked with spruce gum, were as much as 80 feet long. These boats were propelled by long oars or were sometimes provided with sails—another indication of recent migration or continued contact with Asia—made from thin wooden slats or from cedar-bark mats, and could carry crews of twenty men or more. A fire in a box filled with sand, in the center of the hull, provided a cooking place on long voyages. These canoes cruised up and down the coastal waters or sometimes cut across open water from one cape to another.

Women's boats, or family boats, were smaller. They carried the noncombatant members of the household on visits, or from winter house to summer fishing camp. These boats were usually propelled by oars only, without sails, and were not used outside coastal waters.

The great canoes were seldom used for fishing, although the smaller boats were. Fish was the staple of diet, supplemented with wild roots, berries, nuts, acorns, and small game.

The women were endlessly busy: gathering, smoking, and drying food; extracting oil from eulachon, or candlefish, or drying these small fish to string and burn as torches in the great houses on long winter nights; preparing cordage for fishing, mat and basket making, and twining or plaiting the baskets, mats, and blankets. Here basketry developed into as fine a craft as in the Basin-Plateau and California areas.

Some men specialized in fishing or hunting and exchanged their catches with those who had other specialties. Individual and household possessions were stored in cedar-plank boxes, with the planks again steamed, bent, and stitched into place with cedar cord. Often the boxes were elaborately carved and were inlaid with abalone or dentalium shell.

Mountain-sheep-horn spoons were made by the same whittle-steam-bend-and-carve method that was used in working wood. The spoons were seldom decorated otherwise than by carving, and from their designs we can judge the strength and variety of Northwest Coast wood carving before house paints were introduced by the traders and the art became "colorful." Previously, the only colors available had been ocher, hematite, charcoal, and white clay, which enhanced but did not obscure the designs. Trade goods were always desirable to the Indians; the results of their use, by our aesthetics, were not uniformly so.

The high woods pressed down to the shore, enveloping and enclosing the villages and the adjacent graveyards, with their ghostly carved wooden grave markers weathered to a dull gray-black. The mists twined through the woodlands, the ocean swept to the foot of the village, and the people were surrounded by a world that must have seemed both ghostly and ghastly to them, without the sharpness of intense light but with a blending and merging of different degrees of lightlessness, to judge by their myths and ceremonies.

Often in winter the ceremonies, pantomimic enactments of the great myths, went on all night. The participants were robed in blankets and masked, the masks sometimes covering not only the dancer's head but the upper part of his body. There were masks within masks; the great outer cases might be hinged, and at proper moments swung back across the wearers' shoulders to reveal a bear or beaver, perhaps, within a raven or a killer whale.

At the time of a great dance, mat partitions were taken down and the doors of the beds were slid open. The fire was removed from the center of the floor to the back and perhaps a screen was erected between the fire and the wall. The dancers emerged from behind the scene. Members of the audience sat in their places along the side walls.

One shamanistic society identified itself with bears—again animals to be feared and shunned as being protohuman. This society's rituals were at least mock, and sometimes perhaps genuinely cannibalistic. The screen from behind which the impersonators appeared was carved and painted with an enormous bear figure, and it was through his mouth that the dancers stepped. They wore bearskins as costumes, and carved bear masks on their shoulders. Down the center of the long building, growling, crouching, sometimes capering on all fours, the dancers surged. At the climax of their dance they pounced on the man they had selected as their prospective member—or victim—and dragged him back through the screen that hid their lair. There the members realistically devoured their victim, who was thus either initiated or absorbed into their society; sometimes one, and sometimes the other, to judge from the existing accounts.

This was a world of mystery and demons and fear. There was wealth in the forest and the seas, and the Europeans who came to Alaska, Vancouver, and British Columbia grew wealthy and purchased titles and positions as the Indians had.

The Europeans offered the Indians many things besides metal tools and tuberculosis. They brought ribbons and pearl buttons; they brought silver and gold coinage from which men accustomed to working in copper could hammer bracelets and other ornaments; they brought brass kettles to replace the great wooden bowls in which foods had been steamed; they brought red and blue trade cloth and glass beads.

In exchange the Europeans wanted the vast wealth of timber in the forests, the fish, whales, seals, and other mammals that swarmed in the ocean, and little else. They were not interested in settling on the land and plowing the fields their timbering operations had denuded. They were not interested in staying, even as missionaries, until a much later date. There was never the exchange of ideas or of human contacts that inevitably took place in other parts of North America in the same period.

On each side, the world of the Northwest Coast peoples was a world of wealth, and of the terror that great wealth brings to its possessors.

13

Turn to the East

In North American Indian mythology, the four cardinal directions are often called the four world corners. Similarly, most American Indian ceremonies salute the four directions, sometimes including with them three more: up, down, and here—the place where one stands. The latter is, of course, the center of the universe.

The peoples of woodlands and plains, the Yumans and Mohave of the southwestern rivers, the tribes of the Great Basin-Plateau and California areas, and those of the Northwest Coast, all begin at the east, move southward, westward, and so return to the east. The exceptions to this rule are the Pueblo and Athabascan peoples, who begin at the south, move to the west, the north, the east, and so regain the south.

So it is appropriate that having reached the west coast of the continent, coming from the east, to the south, to the west, we turn north and inland, and return to the Atlantic by way of the northern Déné, or Athabascans, and so come again to the Algonkians east and south of them, the people Europeans met first.

Stone carving was an important art of interior Canada in preconquest times, and so was the pecking of pictographs of supernatural and animal figures on standing boulders or the bluffs beside streams.

We have not mentioned pictographs before; the subject is an enormous one and deserves special treatment and much more consideration than we can give it here. In writing of most other culture areas we have had more specimens and documents of other kinds to draw on than we have in the area between the Pacific Ocean and Hudson Bay. One of our main sources of information about the early peoples of this area is the figurines they carved from stone, in the round, or pecked with pointed antlers or pebbles on hard granitic rocks.

In dealing with this vast sweep of country we must depend more on geological reports than on any other written documents. The northern interior of Canada was very little studied by either archaeologists or ethnologists until recent years, and then the fieldwork has most often taken the form of salvage archaeology.

One cause for this hole in the American Indian map is the sheer size of the area. Another is its wide variations in terrain. It has all been mapped now, but for many years whole lakes and mountain ranges got lost between Hudson Bay and the Canadian Rockies. No wonder, then, that the area and its native population have been little and superficially known.

Another reason for our ignorance of the area is that lying as close to the Arctic Circle as it does, the region alternates between the mud and mosquitoes of summer and the bitter cold of winter. The permafrost discourages excavation over much of the area; when its surface thaws, mud is just as difficult to contend with. Until air transportation by helicopter or pontoon planes became possible, there were some parts of northern Canada that could be reached only in winter by dog sled or glimpsed from the boats that made summer runs up the briefly opened rivers. Hence our knowledge of pictographs, which can be studied from the water. And yet, even as this is being written, newspapers and magazines carry reports that the oldest human remains yet disclosed in North America have been found on the southern margin of the region, in a site on the Palouse River in eastern Washington.

This, indeed, was a lucky case of salvage archaeology. In the course of a survey preliminary to the construction of a dam across the Snake River, which will flood many square miles in Idaho and Washington, paleontologist Raold Fryxell and archaeologist Richard Daugherty uncovered bone fragments that had been scraped bare when a bulldozer passed over the site.

That was in 1965. By 1967 the team had sunk a ten-foot shaft and had recovered unmistakably human bone fragments, together with the skeletal remains of game animals. Carbon-14 dating sets their age at 11,000 to 13,000 years old. It is possible that the human bones were the remnants of a cannibal feast, for they had been charred and split as if to extract marrow.

Central Canada is caribou country. The Indians from the Mackenzie and Yukon rivers to the Atlantic coast depended on the caribou as the Indians of the Plains depended on the buffalo. West of Hudson Bay and south of coastal Alaska, the Salishan, Penutian, and Aleut-Eskimo languages were displaced by Athabascan. East of Hudson Bay are Algonquian-speaking peoples. In spite of the linguistic differences, the culture of the area within written history has been remarkably homogeneous.

Caribou-skin tents, shaped like small tipis, were used for shelter in summer, semisubterranean pit houses in winter. Travel was by dog sled, with the dogs specially bred for this purpose. The sled runners were often made of caribou horns, as were the sinew-backed compound bows. All clothing was tailored from caribou skin, with trousers replacing the leggings of the Plains and Atlantic coast peoples for both men and women.

Robes of caribou skins were worn as wraps over soft-tanned caribou-skin shirts. Both robes and shirts might be painted with double-curve designs in soft red and blue earth colors. Here hats were in use, as they were in the Northwest Coast area. Instead of being made of twined and plaited basketry, however, or simply serving as tumpline pads, these were hoods of caribou skin, worn for protection from the intense cold.

Moccasins were bootlike: high, hard-soled, tightly laced up the legs, and often made with the fur side of the skin turned in for winter weather. High bootlike moccasins of a similar pattern were common among the southern Athabascans, and were worn by the southern Plains tribes, the Comanche and Kiowa.

In some ways it is hard to believe that anybody would want to live in this desolate sweep of country, but apparently the northern Athabascans and Algonkians not only lived there; they liked it. And life was not without adornment. The Algonkians of the area were noted for their embroidery in moose hair and porcupine quill on clothing and baskets. Floral designs predominated, although occasionally human or animal figures appeared in the decoration of containers. The northern Cree, before the introduction of glass beads, were particularly facile in such work.

After the French and English discovered that the central Canadian area was rich in furs, "finer than the finest Russian pelts," another lap began in the race between the two European nations to penetrate the inhospitable northern heart of the continent and to exploit it, if not colonize it.

The written history of the north country really is the history of the Hudson's Bay Company. Two Frenchmen, Pierre Radisson and Médard des Groseilliers, penetrated the country by canoe and portage in the mid-seventeenth century, and were astonished and delighted by its wealth of furs, which were almost to be had for the asking. Certainly the pelts were easily secured by trading a metal knife or a handful of glass beads to the Indians. Brandy and rum also made a powerful appeal to trade, even when watered down by 70 percent.

Radisson and Groseilliers at first attempted to interest the French king, Louis XIV, in exploration and development of the country inland from New France proper, but Louis was engaged in war with the Netherlands and had neither men nor money to spare for doubtful overseas ventures.

Refused in France, the two exploiters turned to England, and there found a hospitable reception at the court of Charles II. A stock company was formed and was chartered under the title of The Honourable Hudson's Bay Company. In 1668 the company began to establish trading posts, or factories, on the southern curve of the great bay, which was accessible from the east by water for about four months each year.

Detailed reports and inventories were sent back to England with each shipment of furs out of the area, but narrative reports, when written, were necessarily brief. Beyond the fact that there were Indians in the country, and that the Indians were for many years the principal suppliers of furs to the factories, we know little about them. The Indians hunted, they fished, they trapped, and the women dressed the skins of the animals the men took. There the company's interest in the details of aboriginal life ceased.

That these Indians had complicated languages and kinship systems of their own was not observed until long after trading had become a fact of Indian life. Nor was much note taken of the deftness and skill with which the women made and decorated their garments. The menstrual taboo, observed by all tribes of the area, seems to have escaped the notice of most of the explorers; perhaps the Europeans were simply annoyed because every woman had at least four days' rest from her labors every month. Nor were the first white men aware, apparently, of the Athabascan custom whereby a man did not speak to his mother-in-law, or a woman to her father-in-law or son-in-law. These customs spread, possibly by way of southward-bound Athabascans, to a large part of the Plains, Great Basin, and California areas.

There was no strongly defined social organization among these northern tribes. Their environment dictated that the people live in small, scattered bands, each little village largely sufficient unto itself. The native religion seems to have been a vague thing: a hope for happiness in the hereafter, combined with placation of the dread spirits of cold and famine in the here and now. Life in many ways must have been as bleak and desolate as the landscape. Elaborate ceremonialism was lacking, and there were few myths. Storytelling and oratory were not, apparently, highly developed arts in the north country.

Yet, when England and France went to war again in 1697, it was as much over trade with faraway northern Canada as over any other one thing. Suddenly that barren wilderness of mud and mosquitoes, snow and ice, became vastly desirable, desirable in a way that it would not be again until gold was found along the Yukon in the 1890's, or uranium was discovered in the 1950's.

It was an age of luxury and ostentation in both England and France. The richest furs were in demand to set off the finest jewels and silks at the courts of the two nations. That it had required untold toil on the part of unknown Indian women, and much-told danger and adventure on the part of the traders to procure the furs, mattered not at all to the wealth and nobility of France or England. Their own display of wealth was what counted, and that wealth could be displayed as well in the richness of furs as in the fall of laces and linens.

So we have turned to the east and come again to the Atlantic, and to the European wars that altered the course of history and lives half a world away. We have passed through prehistory with a brief side bow to protohistory. We can begin an account of the forces that shaped Indian lives into the present day: the writing of ethnohistory.

Part Two

Ignorant Armies

14

Tightening Links

HOWEVER MUCH THE EUROPEAN STRUGGLES OF THE SIXteenth, seventeenth, and eighteenth centuries affected the course of history in the New World, however much one series of battles was related to the other, certain significant differences must be kept in mind.

First was the *rationale* for fighting. In the Old World, wars were planned by kings or other great lords, usually for personal aggrandizement. Battles were laid out, troops were disposed, and lines of conflict were drawn up. Then and only then did the troops, mercenaries like their overlords, go into battle. At the end, the survivors on the winning side profited; those on the losing side had a dismal time at best. Wars dragged on for thirty, eighty, a hundred years, until the original cause of the struggle was lost in the mists of time before the conflict was resolved.

The creation of armies of mercenaries had been another result of the rise of the city-states and of the bourgeoisie. In earlier times the lords of the manors or the kingdoms called on their vassals and serfs for fighting men—in effect, a use of draft animals, for the serfs certainly were nothing more. As the middle class grew and strengthened, unemployment increased, and with it the need to absorb surplus men into a changing economy. Paying men to fight was not a new idea—the Roman Legions were a subsidized army. But paying rather than drafting was new; every Roman was expected to give some time to military service under the command of seasoned professional officers.

In the Indian wars of the New World, men on both sides fought, in essence, to defend their homes. The fighting in the French and Indian War did, indeed, mirror the course of war between England and France on the continent, but the men who fought on either side were not fighting as much to advance the cause of two nations overseas as to retain independent control of the country in which they lived and its valuable natural resources. The American Revolution was no accident; mentally and spiritually its leaders were prepared for it long before the Boston Tea Party.

By European standards, the fighting men of the New World were, and were called, rabble. Except in the few cases in the eighteenth century in which mercenaries had been brought overseas and stationed to defend such points as Montreal, Quebec, Strong Point and Ticonderoga, they lacked uniforms, up-to-date armaments, and equipment, and, to the outward eye, any discipline. They had learned from the Indians to fight from ambush, which was considered unsporting by the European professionals. Open-field fighting, with its dramatic and dashing cavalry charges, trumpet calls, and vivid uniforms, was wasted in undergrowth and thickets; even in the eastern woodlands, where the trees grew tall and the forest cover was seldom dense enough to hide a deer from determined eyes, pitched battles were impossible.

Another point to be borne in mind is the common character of the fighters. They were young men, and they were not interested in diplomacy as such. If a conference had to be called and an agreement drawn up, it could be done better after the battle than before. William Bradford, "elder" of Plymouth, was less than sixty when he died. It was precisely his age which had appealed to the younger Pilgrims and led to his standing as their unofficial but recognized statesman.

Survival from infancy had an equal chance with death from ordinary childhood ailments among the colonists. Survival to adulthood was difficult. People married young; both men and women were usually younger than twenty when they married for the first time, and it was taken for granted that the first marriage would not be the last. Childbearing and warfare further reduced the adult population; starvation in bad years and introduced disease cut it down still further.

It is estimated that under the most favorable conditions the total Indian population of America north of Mexico was 600,000 people in the preconquest period. The population controls were the same as those among the whites. Six hundred thousand persons is the size of several contemporary Midwestern cities, including the one in which this is being written. The 600,000 were spread over the subcontinent in varying degrees of density, the highest concentration of population being, of course, in the agricultural areas. From the centers of high technical culture it diminished, until in the northern area, along the Yukon and Mackenzie rivers, population was sparse indeed.

Leaving aside for the moment the low age and survival levels in the non-Indian population, let us think for a moment what their effects were on the Indian population. It can truly be said that youth and the high premium on the lives of members of the in-group determined the development of many Indian cultures.

From infancy an Indian child was precious. Birth might be a relatively easy process, if the mother was of strong constitution and had the help of skillful midwives. Even under contemporary conditions, the death rate of American Indian children under one year of age is double that of the same age group in the general population.

Growing up presented new hazards. Accidents were common. Infectious diseases of European origin had probably been epidemic from time to time since the twelfth century. There was always the danger of capture, for children were preferred captives in many tribes. There was also the possibility of straying from the traveling band or a berrying party and being attacked by wild animals. Outwardly, the life of a preadolescent Indian child was lived in a permissive atmosphere. Actually, it was hedged about with safety restrictions, as those built-in baby-sitters, the grandparents, well knew. Theirs was the task of keeping active children occupied and in groups during much of the day. This was the equivalent of schooling, and it had the same effect as classroom teaching; it gave direction and control to the child's mind.

With the coming of adulthood, the physical life of men in particular became one of declared valor, of courting danger for its own sake. Hunting and warfare alike were risky, and many of the ceremonies held for adolescent boys and young men had as their purpose "to keep them happy, because they may not be with us long." Youth, hard physical conditions, and a mental attitude of daring all contributed to the risks of the young man's life and to reduction of the adult male population.

In consequence, there was an abundance—even a surplus—of females in most tribes. Only in the villages southwest was a more or less static balance between the sexes maintained, and only there was monogamy the accepted pattern for marriage in preconquest times.

The surplus women had to be cared for somehow, and the easiest, quickest, and most natural way of doing so was to marry them off. Usually a man married a first wife when he was about twenty, and he often chose a woman older than himself. Similarly, a woman's first husband usually was older than she. This not only provided homes for widows and widowers; it also served in some measure as a means of personal sex education and training.

A man's plural wives were usually the sisters or the equivalent (mother's sisters' daughters) of the first. A widow most frequently married a brother or the equivalent (father's brothers' sons) of her first husband. It was felt that the sororate and levirate, to use the technical terms, helped to hold families together and prevent friction among the children of multiple marriages. Very often children passed from hand to hand, from one "mother" to another, until they were surer of the identity of their biological fathers than of their biological mothers.

For a woman, the onset and progress of the childbearing years were burdened with extra precautions, restrictions, and supernatural dangers. The beginning of the menstrual period, in many tribes, led to a series of taboos. These began with a ceremony which publicly announced a girl as physically ready for marriage. This was followed by monthly seclusion in a small structure away from the family dwelling, the eating of or abstaining from certain foods, the avoidance of salt, and usually the use of a small pointed stick instead of the fingers for scratching.

A similar separate building housed a woman during and after childbirth, when she was under the same restrictions that marked her menstrual periods. There was no rite to mark the passage that has become the one most frequently socially observed in our culture, the onset of menopause, probably because few women survived to reach that time of life.

In most Indian tribes an individual was mature at twenty, a ripe elder at thirty-five, and aged before fifty. Anything less like twentieth-century America's cult of youth would be difficult to conceive. Perhaps in our terms the best possible summary is the flippant phrase, "You should live so long."

The age-level factor was equally clear with the invading Europeans, as we have said. Auguste Chouteau was sent up the Mississippi in command of a flotilla of his godfather's trade boats and instructed to establish a trading post at the confluence of the Mississippi and Missouri rivers when he was thirteen. St. Louis is his monument. Lafayette was twenty when he assumed command of a division of the Continental Army. Thomas Jefferson penned the Declaration of Independence, with all its astute reasoning and sonorous phrases, when he was in his mid-thirties.

We repeat, on either side, it was a young person's world, held steady and balanced by such elders as Benjamin Franklin and Red Jacket, but a world of action that only the young could supply, when the Thirteen Atlantic Colonies broke with England and began shaping themselves into the United States.

15

Matters of Policy

BEFORE WE PROCEED ANY FURTHER ALONG THE WESTward course of empire, it might be well to consider the three national policies that helped to guide its way. Because of differences in points of view about colonial administration, Spain, France, and England pursued very distinct policies of developing the newly opened continent.

The Spanish policy was relatively simple: convert the Indians, use them, and otherwise leave them alone. Upper-class Spaniards might take Indian concubines, for lack of other women, but the Spaniards lived always on the surface of the land, developing and exploiting it and sending the fruits of success back to Mexico or Spain.

The *paisanos* who were imported to develop the agricultural areas of New Spain learned from and taught the Indians. Never having been rich, the *peons* looked forward to the achievement not of riches but of a living. The Indians had successfully cultivated the soil for centuries, and they and the Spanish peasants exchanged ideas and techniques on an almost unconscious level. The agriculturalists lived side by side, never blending into a single population, instead remaining separate but equal in most ways.

The French were primarily explorers and exploiters, but in a different way. Spanish colonial administration began with Spanish exploration and conquest. The French cagily delayed the actual processes of government until they were sure there was something in the New World that was worth governing. The first Frenchmen were of the bourgeoisie, unemployed and restless in Europe, and willing to face the risks of New France with the same bravado with which they had faced the armies of Spain and England in the Netherlands.

The French, too, took Indian concubines, but they also took Indian wives. By the first quarter of the eighteenth century French names were spread up and down the Mississippi Valley: Bienville, La Harpe, Laclède, Chouteau, Roubidoux, La Flesche—the list is a long one. Half-French, half-Indian families established themselves as leaders and intermediaries among groups. New France was bounded on the west by the Pacific Ocean, according to French claims, for they ignored the overlapping of other colonial empires. More than any other nation, the French developed the heart of the country, and they did it with a minimum of displacement of native populations.

The French policy of peaceful coexistence with the Indians did not prevent some sharp conflicts between the parties. More frequently, however, Indians became involved in the struggle between the French and the English, on one side or the other, as each nation enlisted Indian allies.

Until the mid-eighteenth century, and then only in restricted areas, the French colonials were not farmers. They, like the Indians among whom they had settled, were hunters, trappers, and fishermen. They harvested timber for sale in France, it is true, and they made some small attempt to develop the lead and copper mines around the Great Lakes, where the metals occurred in almost pure form.

Because the Indians the French knew best were woodsmen and rivermen, and were willing to trade with the French trappers and hunters, it was possible to enlist Indians to fight against the English. The French and Indian War in North America was only a shadow of the conflict that tore Europe apart in the seven years between 1756 and 1763. The English victory overseas ended French colonialism as such in the New World, by expropriating all French lands to England.

Neither Spanish nor French attitudes, then, had much to do with shaping the policy of the new nation that was fumbling to be formed along the Atlantic seaboard. That policy was based almost entirely on English colonialism.

Primarily, the great quality of the English was that they had come to stay. Merchants, craftsmen, landless younger sons, scholars, clergymen, and jurists all arrived in North America with the intention of reproducing English social structure as best they might. The king of England was also king of New England and Virginia. It might be a hard struggle, carried forward under difficult conditions, but the fact that there would always be an England and that this was an extension of it was never long out of the minds of "the loyal subjects over the seas."

The establishment of the Cromwellian Commonwealth did little to affect the course of English colonial history. Communication was slow; the social structure in the English colonies was functioning, and while the men of Massachusetts welcomed the rise of the Lord Protector, the men of Virginia were horrified by the assassination of the king. It is conceivable that this difference of attitudes was the first seed sown in the conflict that was harvested in the Civil War a century later.

Differences of opinion among the colonists had nothing to do with the Indians. What mattered was that the Indians occupied good farmland and the English wanted to farm. From the first winter, the Pilgrims went armed, even though they consistently reported that the Indians were not aggressive against them, even when the founding fathers stole the Indians' seed corn.

The settlers of the northern colonies were fundamentally men of the cities, again of the rising middle class. Agriculture came hard to them; they had to learn about it. The *Mayflower,* when she returned to England from her first voyage out, carried wood, furs, and a little salt fish—together with pleas for flour and wheat.

In Virginia and the Carolinas living was easier but the first agricultural exports were almost entirely tobacco and additional cargoes of timber. As the woods were cut down, settlement moved inward, pushing the Indians ahead of the advancing farmers.

It is easy to romanticize the plantation life of the south, both before and after the Revolution. A few men did become wealthy, as large landowners and owners of slaves. But the bulk of the southern settlers and planters were farmers on a much smaller scale, who owned few or no slaves, who toiled from "cain see to cain't see," much as their descendants do today. These were the frontiersmen of the south—not discoverers, explorers, or exploiters, but dirt farmers. They and their like had as much to do with shaping southern history as did the great planters of the seaboard and Piedmont areas.

Where the northern woodlands swept away, open and clear of tangled underbrush in the main, from the Atlantic to the Great Lakes, the mountains rose steeply behind the southern plantations. Here there was no easy way out, geographically, for the Indians. They could not withdraw before white encroachment into a more or less familiar type of environment. The southern Indians had to move away from the rivers and the more open woodlands into the highlands, where no strangers wanted to come as yet.

Eliminate or push aside, then, was the English policy. Make treaties—the number is astronomical—and when the land is legally secure in white man's hands, develop it—and make more treaties. The process could, apparently, be continued *ad infinitum*. There was always land and more land, and all it took was another piece of paper to secure what the Englishmen wanted.

In the last analysis, it was not the dour dominance of the Spaniards, or the blithe laissez-faire of the French, that shaped the course of North American Indian history. It was the brush-aside-and-override, divide-and-conquer agriculturalism of the English.

The first treaty of the "United States of North-America" with an Indian tribe was entered into with the "Delaware Nation of Indians," September 17, 1778. The United States was at war with England, and had been for two years. The Constitutional Convention would not meet in Philadelphia until 1787. But the Continental Congress was convened, and it sent out Commissioners Andrew and Thomas Lewis to deal with Captain White Eyes, Captain John Kill Buck, Jr., and Captain Pipe, the delegates and the chief men of the Delawares, and to sign a treaty drawn as between two sovereign nations.

Article III of the treaty specified that the Delawares did "hereby stipulate and agree to give a free passage through their country to the troops . . . and the same to conduct by the nearest and best ways to the posts, forts or towns of the enemies of the United States. . . ."

Article IV continued, "For the better security of the peace and friendship now entered into . . . neither party shall proceed to the inflictions of punishments on the citizens of the other. . . ."—a recognition of status which was to cause endless legal involvements between both parties in later years.

The British were meanwhile busy signing treaties of their own. Precedent, after all, was with them. The principal one was that with the Six Nations of the Iroquois. In 1784, one year after the Treaty of Paris had marked the conclusion of the Revolution, the new United States Congress being assembled, sent out Commissioners Plenipotentiary Oliver Wolcott, Richard Butler, and Arthur Lee to sign a separate peace treaty with the "Sachems and Warriors of the Six Nations," which would supersede the Nations' previous treaties with England.

Treaty making with Indian tribes as with separate and independent nations continued until 1871. In that year, by the Act of March 3, all treaties were abolished, and the Indians were brought "under the protection of the United States."

During this period of almost a century, titles to Indian lands rested in tribal hands. A tribe might be diminished—almost extinguished—by disease, intermarriage, or removal, but still, as a tribe, it held title to certain lands. Titles were not extinguished by "acts of conquest" on the part of the United States, but always with at least token agreement from the Indians.

Most treaties included clauses of peace and amnesty—and of payment for ceded lands in cash or kind. This was an effective means of improving the divide-and-rule method of handling ticklish situations, for if one faction within a tribe would not sign a treaty, another would—and would thereupon reap the material benefits of being good little Indians.

Somewhere through the almost two centuries that have passed since the first treaty was signed with the Delawares, a poetic expression has come into being. It is popularly believed, by Indians and whites alike, that treaties were signed to endure for "as long as the grass shall grow and the rivers shall run." This is an appealing piece of folklore, probably originally coined by a vote-getting politician. An actual check of the treaty texts, as contained in *Indian Affairs: Laws and Treaties*, Vol. II (Treaties), as compiled by Charles J. Kappler, clerk to the Senate Committee on Indian Affairs, in 1904, has failed to disclose the romantic phrase in the text of any Indian treaty.

There is no other expression in the contemporary vocabulary that has caused more trouble and confusion. Did "as long as the grass shall grow" mean "until the prairies are plowed and planted to crops and the earth rises in dust smoke against the sky"? Did "as long as the rivers shall run" mean "until the rivers are dammed and their waters spread over lakes"? The nonexistent phrases have been and are subject to a vast variety of interpretations, none of them complimentary to the Secretaries of the Interior or commissioners of Indian Affairs of the United States. In 1968, 300 Indians from all parts of the

United States convened in Henryetta, Oklahoma, once again trying to recapture "treaty rights" that were abrogated and abolished by the Act of 1871. The path of history seldom runs smooth or straight, but in this case it is somewhat bumpier and more crooked than usual.

Actually, the provisions of the treaties, and later of the agreements between the United States government and various Indian groups, tended to deal less and less with the material rewards of virtue and more and more with such practical, shared benefits as schools, health care, improved administration, law and order, road construction, and soil conservation. Blacksmiths and school teachers alike were provided at government expense, and sometimes the same person served in both capacities. Specialization increased as time went on, and in 1968 the Bureau of Indian Affairs had an administrative budget of more than $2,000,000. It is the biggest single employer of Indians in the United States, for it gives them preferential treatment in Civil Service examinations.

Before the present situation was reached, there were many halts and retreats, many contradictions and betrayals, on both sides.

"The road to civilization," observed Thomas Wildcat Alford, a Shawnee and a graduate of Carlisle Indian School, to his biographer in the 1920's, "has not always been easy for us poor savages."

16

Tears Along the Trails

THE MOVEMENT INLAND, ALONG THE RIVERS AND UP into the hills, was as slow—almost imperceptible—as the change of cultures among the southeastern Indian tribes.

As the Indians gave way before the advancing English colonists, tribes merged with stronger tribes, confederacies became more and more closely united, some languages disappeared, and others blended with one another. It was a time for survival of the fittest, and the fittest were not those who fought hardest and invited extermination. The fittest were those whose adaptability and mental flexibility could carry them through a time of crisis without overt struggle.

In the 1770's naturalist William Bartram had noted that many of the Indians lived "as well if not better" than the majority of white frontiersmen. As Bartram's travels carried him southward, the Indians he encountered grew "wilder," although nowhere was he threatened or treated badly. In part this must have been due to Bartram's own personality. His account of his journey shows him to have been a gentle man, truly fascinated by the new plants and animals he encountered and truly eager to learn what he could from the medicine men and "wise sages" among the Indians. Bartram learned much, not only about the plants and animals but about the peoples of the southeast, and his are the fullest and most reliable accounts of daily life among them that we have from this period.

One great force that had been at work to change the life pattern of the southeastern Indians was the pack peddlers. The country was not always open for river travel, and the English traders were never the waterborne explorers that the French were. In fact, the English traders were not explorers at all, in the sense of having set forth "for to admire and for to see." They were men of business, and if business could most effectively be transacted from the backs of pack ponies, so it was.

Ponies and mules, small and surefooted, sometimes in long trains of animals, sometimes only one or two herded along by a single man, went everywhere along the Atlantic coast and into the Piedmont, traversed the paths of the foothills, and finally scrambled along the ridges of the Alleghenies.

In the packs on their animals' backs the traders loaded a truly impressive inventory. If the account of Oñate's setting forth reads like the prize list at a state fair, the inventories of the pack peddlers read like those of discount houses. Rum if the trader was English; brandy if he was French—the liquor watered down regardless of nationality. Knives, axes, saws, hammers, and hatchets. Long rifles, black powder, and molds and lead for making balls. Cotton: calico, muslin, sacking, duffels, and lace. Ribbons, jewelry, and mirrors. Brass kettles and water jugs; tools and rivets and solder to repair the vessels if they broke or wore out. Dishes, linens, kerchiefs, table forks, and spoons.

And beads, especially beads. These were made in Venice, first for the slave traders setting out for Africa, later for the Indian trade. The beads, which came to be known as pony beads because of the way they were distributed, were relatively large, nearly a sixteenth of an inch in diameter. The colors were limited: black, white, yellow, blue and green, and a specially blown, much-desired garnet red, its interior coated with white. Beads were heavy to carry, and correspondingly valuable.

Sometimes the traders traveled with Indian guides; sometimes they made their way alone, depending on the stars, the slope of the hills, and the personal sense of direction for guidance. Wherever and however they went, the traders were welcome, for they were great gossips—almost as great as the missionaries—and they could be relied on to bring news.

Sometimes a trader married into an Indian family and settled down in Indian country. These were the first millers, the first saw wrights, and the first tavernkeepers. Sometimes a trader lived with an Indian wife for a year or two and moved on, returning when and as the spirit moved him. Both groups contributed to the growing part-blood population of the southeast.

More and more the part bloods rose to have power and influence. They were bilingual, in most cases. Many of them inherited considerable property from their non-Indian fathers. In some cases a half- or quarter-blood youngster was sent north to school, and many colleges and academies established scholarship funds for Indian students. Yale, Harvard, Columbia, William and Mary, Dartmouth, and Cornell are among the Ivy League colleges which continue the institution to this day.

The influence of the missionaries for change was as great as that of the traders. This was the time of an upheaval within the Anglican Church. John and Charles Wesley were setting out, with their associates, to introduce the "Method" of Christianity to laborers and miners in England. Eventually John Wesley and Francis Asbury, both still ordained Anglican priests, came to Virginia and the Carolinas, where they not only preached to those farmers and workingmen who were too poor to contribute to the support of a state church, but even to slaves and Indians.

The German Moravians, an offshoot of Lutheran Protestantism, proved as zealous and effective as the Methodists. Their missionary John Heckewelder worked among the Delaware Indians. He has left us the only even partially complete account of Delaware life before it was drastically changed by outside pressures.

The Presbyterians moved into the mission field about the end of the eighteenth century and were particularly well received by the Chickasaw and the Choctaw. The Cherokee and Creek had welcomed the Moravians and encouraged them to set up schools, to which all children within walking distance were welcome. The three R's were drilled into small Cherokee and Creek heads long before the turn of the century.

Wealthy mixed-blood planters of all tribes formed an aristocracy of their own and employed private tutors for their children. Lands, fields, and houses were in no way different from those of the non-Indians. The upper class owned slaves, and the whole social and economic pyramid rested on sweating black backs. Horses and livestock were thoroughbred. Racing, gambling, and drinking were as frequent among the wealthy Indians as among the Tidewater plantation owners. Men, and sometimes women, made trips north or overseas to see and be seen, to shop, to visit, to play politics. There were large libraries and elegant clothing and fine food in many southeastern Indian homes. In no sense of the word were these painted savages, and in that much they were a disappointment to strangers.

True, the wealthy upper class was only a small percentage of the total Indian population, as it had always been. It was sufficiently leisured and educated to take an active part in politics, both tribal and international, for it must be remembered that these nations of Indians dealt with European nations and with the United States on equal terms. The Cherokee and Choctaw for a time maintained ambassadors at the Court of St. James's. And they were shrewd ambassadors, capable of dealing with world politics when the necessity arose.

The old pattern of tribal government was maintained: a Principal Chief, a House of Kings (corresponding to our Senate), and a House of Warriors (corresponding to our House of Representatives). It cannot be honestly said that the men who comprised the governing bodies of the Cherokee, Creek, Chickasaw, and Choctaw actually represented the lower classes. They spoke for the small farmers and craftsmen, and theirs were the voices that were heard. This was the way it always had been, and this was the way it always would be.

Not all Indians in the southeast welcomed the missionaries, or attended schools, and not all of them accepted Christianity. The old town dance grounds persisted, each surrounded with seven shelters, or beds; one for each clan. The old ceremonies were still performed and were well attended. The ceremonial stickball play went on, and many mixed-blood young men participated in it. Native languages were still spoken; poems and songs and prayers were still composed; native doctors practiced their old ways of healing.

A stir was in the air and change was coming. There was little, materially, to distinguish the average middle-income Indian home from a comparable non-Indian one, but the two were still far apart in language and in habits of thinking. The non-Indian usually had gone into the Indian nations to make his fortune, while the full-blood asked only to be left alone to enjoy what he had.

This was the situation when, early in the nineteenth century, traders began to bring down bird quills filled with gold dust from the Cherokee hills. Pelts, dried meat and fish, cornmeal, and tobacco had been the principal exports from the Cherokee country before. Now there was gold, fulfilling the rumors that had started with De Soto's men and been sustained by occasional nuggets from upstream but never quite confirmed or located.

The discovery of gold came at a critical period in Cherokee history. The hill-country half-breed Sequoyah had fought against the British in the War of 1812. He had seen men in the United States Army receive letters from home; the marks on the talking leaves spoke to the men and gave them news of their families and communities.

If white men could do it, Cherokee could, Sequoyah decided. Single-handed, illiterate in the English which he did not even speak, he set out to find a way by which Indians could communicate with one another across the miles. And he did it. He invented a phonetic syllabary, the only such invention of a single man in human history.

Sequoyah took his invention to the tribal council, bringing his daughter (Ahyokah—She Brought It) with him. While her father waited outside the council house, the twelve-year-old set down the dictation of the Principal Chief, John Ross. Then Sequoyah, recalled to the council, read back what the child had written. A miracle had happened. Cherokee could read and write. Within three months every capable person in the Cherokee Nation was literate in the Sequoyah syllabary. Each taught another, and the knowledge ran like wildfire up the hills and along the ridges. People wrote letters to each other and carried them to the recipients by hand, for the pure joy of a shared experience.

Now that there was a way of reading, the Cherokee wanted something to read. The missionaries had previously attempted translations of the Bible but had been balked by the problem of designating the pitches of a tonal language. Now they need not translate it. Types were ordered cast in Boston, a press was purchased, and the Cherokee printing press went into business at the national capital, Echota, with the Gospel According to St. Matthew and a newsletter, *The Cherokee Phoenix*. There was a national school system. There were plans for a national academy and museum. There was a national pension, in the form of a salt bed, for Sequoyah—the only pension awarded for intellectual achievement in United States history.

Even before Sequoyah's time, some Cherokee had grown fearful of non-Indian encroachment and had begun to shift west into Arkansas and Oklahoma. A few even went as far south as the new Republic of Mexico. Sam Houston, who had lived with the Cherokee between 1829 and 1833, and was well liked and respected by them, suggested the southward movement. After his upper-class Cherokee wife, Talihina, or Diana Rogers, died, Houston left the Nation and went south to join Moses Austin's settlers in the lands along the Brazos River. This northern portion of the Mexican Republic, known as Texas after a Caddoan tribe native to the area, was beginning to talk of breaking away from Mexico. Houston encouraged Cherokee settlers to join the colony that was forming around the Spanish community known as San Antonio.

The combination of Austin's Anglo settlers and the Mexican natives produced tensions and pressures of its own, many of which were diverted against the Cherokee. Within a short time most of the Indians shook the dust of Texas from their feet and went north to relatively unsettled and untroubled Arkansas. Here they formed a nucleus around Forts Smith and Gibson, where in time they became known as the Old Settlers.

Sequoyah himself was one of them, and they had learned to read and write before the Nation East had. The Old Settlers addressed themselves, in the Sequoyah syllabary, to friends and relatives at home and begged them to come out to the Nation West. Some accepted the invitation. Most of the Cherokee simply did not believe that further change was coming upon them. They did not realize how great or how many were the changes they had already experienced. Conservative by nature, the hill Cherokee in particular clung to their homelands.

Come out, the Old Settlers begged their friends and relatives. Come out to this no-man's land, which no European country claims and which the United States has not thought about. The hills rise rolling here, like the hills at home. The streams are clear; game and fish are abundant and easily taken. There are good farmlands here, in the bottoms. There are even some traders, so you will not lack your little luxuries. Nobody lives here but ignorant savages, the Osage and the Quapaw, and they have few guns and don't want to make trouble for other Indians. Come out, and be safe.

Safe the western country might be, but it was a long way away from the uplands of Tennessee, the Carolinas, and Georgia. Few ventured the long journey by cart or wagon, or on the riverboats that had been moving along the Mississippi and its tributaries since 1811. It was too far, the eastern Cherokee protested. Too far from anything they knew and loved. Yes, they missed their friends and relatives. But at least they were at home.

The problem of states' rights entered the question. Were treaties made by the federal government binding upon the separate states? If the Constitution said they were, then was the Constitution constitutional? What was there to prevent the states' militia from going in and clearing out the pesky redskins, once and for all, if the federal troops did not?

To cap it all, Old Hickory Andrew Jackson, mumbling his false teeth in the White House while he brooded over insults gratuitously offered his wife, was an inveterate Indian fighter. If he did not himself say that the only good Indian was a dead one, he certainly would have agreed with the later general who did. Yes, he had enlisted Indian troops against the British, and the Cherokee had fought with distinction against their tribal enemies and the British allies, the Creek, at the battles of Horseshoe Bend and New Orleans. But those Indian troops were irregulars, long since paid off, disbanded, and sent home. What did the nation as a whole, or any of its states, owe the Indians in the 1830's.

And so the final process began. Divide and conquer. Set the full bloods against the mixed bloods; divide the mixed bloods by power wrangles among themselves. Above all, get somebody, by any device at all, to sign a treaty. That would make the whole thing legal. The Indians could then be removed to lands in the west, beyond the frontier, in a perfectly honest, outright, and legal fashion. Those who resisted, of course, would be revolutionaries, traitors, and subject to shooting and capture.

It was done. The old blood feuds, older than the first European settlements, were revived. The old tribal political divisions were encouraged. Parties and factions were formed, each with its blind and largely dumb adherents among the lower classes, who would suffer equally whatever party was in power. Some of the chiefs touched the pens and signed the papers. Removal was inevitable. Tribal leaders had sanctioned it. In 1835 removal began.

Militiamen rode through the Indian country, burning and looting. Some chose the homesites they would occupy when the Indians were gone. Others simply destroyed what they could not immediately use. Women going out to feed their chickens; men and boys working the fields; young girls busy with household chores—all were driven before the local troops, down to the mouths of the rivers, where concentration camps waited to receive them.

The horrors of those camps will never be forgotten. Disease, starvation, and filth haunted them, leaving death where their shadows had passed. Shelter and food alike were lacking. Water was polluted. There was no means of sanitation. Clothing soon wore out, and the proud people huddled in their rags.

Theoretically, the removal of the southeastern Indians was under the direction of the United States Army, which was responsible for transportation and for maintenance, for the health and clothing of the people en route. The camps were under the supervision of the local militia. Red tape became hopelessly snarled. People who should have been evacuated in early May were barely under way in late November.

The routes varied, but the overall pattern of removal did not. Flatboats or keelboats on the Tennessee, the Hiwassee, the Tombigbee, and other rivers took the people to the Mississippi, where they transferred to other vessels. Some went overland directly from their second landing points; others, like most of the Cherokee, were moved upriver to a railhead, traveled by the new steamcars to a point where river transportation was again possible, and then made their way from the upstream landing to their new territory.

Still others, lucky ones, drove their own teams and wagons, or hitched up their oxcarts, and carried families and household goods over the traders' trails to the west. And still others, least lucky of all, simply walked, trudging up mountain paths and slogging through Arkansas mud day after day. They buried their dead where the weakest dropped beside the trails, and they went on.

The more devoted missionaries went with the Indians, afoot or on horseback, giving what help and comfort they could. Samuel Austin Worcester, missionary to the Cherokee, loaded the Cherokee press in one wagon, the fonts of type in another, and a few bound books in the syllabary into his buggy when he and his family set out. In 1836 building began at Park Hill, in what is now eastern Oklahoma. Thanks to Worcester, the Cherokee press could be reset and printed in the Nation West.

Army doctors were outspoken in their denunciation of the conditions in the camps and along the roads. The doctors were on hand primarily to care for the troops, but their actual practice included prenatal care, deliveries, and such postnatal care as could be rendered. The physicians tended patients with malaria, pneumonia, smallpox, cholera, measles, gunshot wounds, broken limbs, and all the other assorted ailments to which human flesh is heir.

By the time they reached their destinations the tribes were decimated. From prosperous, and sometimes wealthy, people they had become paupers. Those who survived had endured torments and humiliations unequalled in modern history before the twentieth century.

In writing this chapter we have dealt largely with the Cherokee. Every tribe at some time or other had its trail of tears. The Cherokee were not alone. Probably the Creek suffered more; certainly their agony was equal to that of their northern neighbors. The Caddo and their affiliated tribes, who were moved out of Texas a few years later, endured similar suffering—and their story is still to be told.

The Cherokee were a literate and articulate people, as they are today. They could write their own history. And they were singularly fortunate in the doctors and officers who traveled with them and left their own diaries, letters, and accounts of the Cherokee removal. The story of the Cherokee is only one of many, but it is the most thoroughly documented and best known. For that reason it has been selected as the type example of Indian removals from the southeast.

A word should be added about the westward movement of the Choctaw and Chickasaw. These tribes had long held the balance of power between the French and Spanish, from the Mississippi delta north almost to the mouth of the White River.

Inveterate traders, the people traveled north and west, as far as the Wabash in one direction and the Staked Plains of the Texas Panhandle in the other. When the small eastern woodland buffalo had been eliminated, and all other game had grown scarce, the Choctaw and Chickasaw traded with the Osage, Ponca, Kaw, Quapaw, and even with those loners of the Plains, the Pawnee, for buffalo hides, beaver and muskrat pelts, and other skins which they, in turn, exchanged with the French and Spanish traders along the Mississippi. In the course of these transactions, both Choctaw and Chickasaw had an opportunity to view the western lands and to appraise the country, even without a conscious eye to later settlement.

The end result was, in the case of the Chickasaw particularly, that when the time came to go, the people went with a goal. They had sent men ahead to inspect the land in the western territory—not young men, like the scouts for a war party, but seasoned elders with an eye to farm and grazing lands—and when the Chickasaw were ready to go, they went. They paid the expenses of their own removal, and they paid the expenses of travel and resettlement. Alone of the Civilized Tribes the Chickasaw did not travel a trail of tears.

The Choctaw, and particularly the poor people among them, suffered almost as intensely as the Cherokee and Creek. Settled in the swampy, malarial southern part of Indian Territory (now eastern Oklahoma), along the Arkansas and Texas borders, the Choctaw never recovered completely from the pangs of removal. Even though the tribal leaders were prepared themselves, and tried to prepare and reassure their people, most Choctaw did no more than squeeze a living from the marshy, hookworm-plagued lands where they were settled.

The pattern of Indian removals, once set, changed little for almost three-quarters of a century. Once land became desirable, it was possessed. The original owners were moved, and agreement followed treaty, by each of which the Indians gave up portions of their lands for resettlement of other tribes, until Indian country shrank almost to the vanishing point.

17

The Lingerers

NOT ALL MEMBERS OF ANY GIVEN TRIBE MOVED WEST out of the southeast. Small isolated population pockets remained, hidden in hills, woods, and swamplands.

Even though they remained on their original lands, these people were indeed the dispossessed. They held no title to land as individuals, and tribal titles had been extinguished by the preremoval treaties. Educational, health, and other benefits available to the majority of their tribesmen were not open to them. The whites despised them; as former slaveholders, they did not consider the Negroes their equals; and they hung in a marginal, never-never land, too poor to fight and too weak to assert themselves.

Only one southeastern Indian group had the courage and determination—and natural environment—which made defiance possible. These people were first called by their Creek name: Samano, or runaways. Later the name became Anglicized to Seminole. In time, the Seminole become the fifth of the Five Civilized Tribes.

Actually, the Seminole were no more a tribe than they were civilized in the dictionary sense of "living in cities." They were small groups of people, the remnants of many tribes and bands. They had taken refuge in the swamplands of central and southern Florida, where deer were still plentiful and where nobody but themselves seemed likely to want to go. The Seminole hunted and fished. They found the raised "hammocks" of earth that were a foot or so higher than the surrounding swamps, and on the hammocks they clustered their villages, each one housing,

Woman on Horseback with Baby in Cradle Accompanied by Son. Kiowa year count by Bird-Tied-on-Top-of-His-Head, Ft. Marion, Florida. 1871—Plate 20.

Fairfield Museum and Planetarium, St. Johnsbury, Vermont.

Wooden headpiece, part of protective armor. Tlingit. Northwest Coast, 1870.

Courtesy American Museum of Natural History, New York.

Bella Coola grave-post. Northwest Coast, 1870.

Courtesy American Museum of Natural History, New York.

Grave-post from Vancouver Island. Kwakiutl, 1880.

Courtesy American Museum of Natural History, New York.

Bella Coola Indian mask, Northwest Coast, 1890.

Courtesy American Museum of Natural History, New York.

Carved horn spoon used by Tlingit Indians, 1890. Two views.

Courtesy American Museum of Natural History, New York.

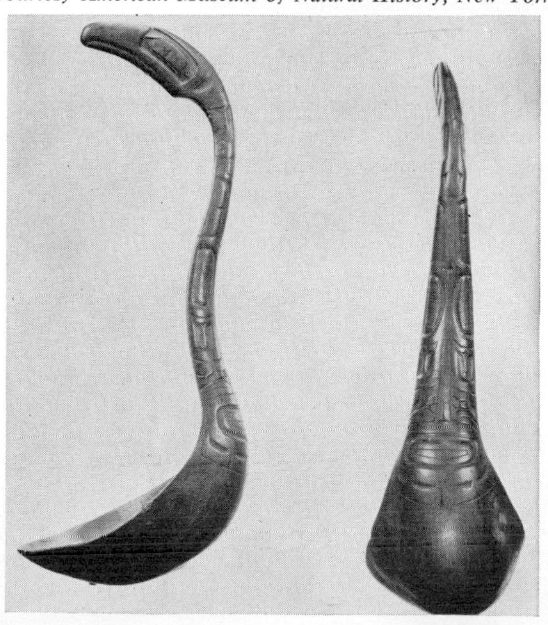

Haida masks. Northwest Coast, 1890.

Courtesy American Museum of Natural History, New York.

Model group illustrating Hopi Snake Dance. Arizona, 1890.

Courtesy American Museum of Natural History, New York.

Sequoyah. Portrait by Charles Banks Wilson. Oklahoma State Capitol Building.

Courtesy Oklahoma State Board of Affairs.

Jim Thorpe, "Athlete of the half-century." Portrait by Charles Banks Wilson. Oklahoma State Capitol Building.

Courtesy Oklahoma State Board of Affairs.

Wooden comb. Tlingit. Northwest Coast, 1908. Carving represents a bear sitting on its haunches.

Courtesy American Museum of Natural History, New York.

Kiowa Gourd Clan Powwow. July 2, 3, 4, 1960. "A Giveaway."

Courtesy Marriott-Rachlin.

Kiowa man asleep. Oklahoma, 1960.

Courtesy Marriott-Rachlin.

Grandfather, priest, teacher. Shipaulovi, Arizona, 1962.

Courtesy Marriott-Rachlin.

On the Kiva steps. San Ildefonso Pueblo, New Mexico, 1964.
Courtesy Marriott-Rachlin.

Blackfoot chief in Northern-style headdress. Wyoming, 1957.

in palmetto-thatched, open-sided chikees the members of an extended family.

Here, in isolation made more complete by the surrounding Anglo-American culture, the last remnants of the great circum-Caribbean culture endured into the twentieth century. Two constellations of settlement formed; one around Lake Okeechobee, in the central part of the state, and the other at the southern tip of the peninsula, in the Big Cypress Swamp.

The Seminole existed under tribal law. It was their proud boast that, although their leaders had once surrendered to the United States Army, they had never signed a peace treaty. The Seminole liked to refer to themselves as "renegades."

Some were captured at the time of the Creek removal and were moved into the western part of the Indian Territory, but as many more escaped deeper into the swamps and hid. Runaway slaves joined them, as did some outlawed white men. The Seminole were hospitable; they took in all comers and gave them shelter.

Thus a blended culture rose; not Creek, Mikasuki, Mobilian, Biloxi, or Araucanian, although it contained elements of all. It was uniquely Seminole. Creek was spoken by the northern group; Mikasuki by the southern, but the material culture and general pattern of life was the same for both.

In general, Seminole culture derived from and rested on a basis of wood—generally cypress. The chikees, which were at once shelters and beds, were built of cypress poles and thatched with palmetto fans. Large, poled dugout canoes, drawing only an inch or so of water, were burned out of cypress trunks. The men poled their way through the rank water weeds growing in the bayous in search of fish, deer, and, later, alligators.

Baskets were plaited or woven from palmetto fronds. Bowls and spoons were carved from cypress wood. Pottery was not made, but metal tools and utensils, obtained from traders on the men's rare forays out of the swamps, were used. So was cotton fabric, which was made into long sweeping dresses for the women and tuniclike shirts for the men. At first these garments were made of strips of plain colored cloth; later, the colored fabrics were torn or cut into fragments, and the garments were made, as they still are, of strips of patchwork. Silver coins were hammered and cut to make filigree ornaments for the women's dresses.

Seminole social control rested with the older men, who were equally priests and headmen. They advised and instructed, and occasionally imposed punishments, but they were not chiefs in the sense of being rulers.

Seminole religion is little known, beyond the bare fact that a native religion still exists and is still practiced. Here, as had happened earlier in the southwest, native religion "went underground" to evade non-Indian criticism and interference. There are dance grounds hidden away in the swamps, and a sacred fire still burns—somewhere—but these are Seminole secrets and are jealously guarded.

The Seminole were fortunate. The Huma and Chitimacha in Louisiana; the Choctaw and Creek in Alabama and Mississippi; the Cherokee in North Carolina, and the Koasati and Alibamu in southeastern Texas were less fortunate.

These people were literally men without countries. They lacked even the shadow of protection conferred by treaty rights. They fell between two races and were despised and rejected by both. Poverty, disease, and ignorance haunted them, for their children were not admitted to "white" schools or to the "separate but equal" schools of the Negroes. It was more than a century before their ethnic existence was acknowledged.

All these remnants of tribes made some basketry, and the women contributed to family support by the sale of baskets and dolls. The men were day laborers—when they could find work. Huddled in wattle-daub cabins, the stay-at-homes waited out the years, until at last their existence and their needs were recognized.

Other lingerers remained along the north Atlantic coast, clinging to the beaches or cranberry bogs, where they could manage to get by—barely. Some of them intermarried with Portuguese fishermen and others with Negro deckhands and cooks. Like the southern Indians, these remnant Passamaquoddy, Nanticoke, Mohegan, and Narragansett formed a huddled world of their own, not quite a part of that which surrounded them.

Still the northern left-behinds kept up their languages and some of their old customs. They still exchanged strings and belts of wampum beads among themselves as pledges of good faith.

Once most of the coastal Indians made and used wampum, which consisted of strands of tubular beads ground from the columella of the quahog clam. These beads were white, but there was also a purple wampum, laboriously ground and shaped from the lip of the clamshell. True wampum beads are a quarter to a half inch long and proportionately small in diameter.

At the time of the first white landfalls, the Narragansett brought strings of wampum into Plymouth as pledges of their good faith in their dealings with the colonists. When the whites noticed the value that the Indians placed on wampum, they decided that it was the Indian equivalent of their own money and could be used to purchase needed objects.

Actually, wampum was not a medium of exchange. It was a declaration of friendship and loyalty. The white referred to the pure heart of the giver, and the blue or purple to the honesty of his intentions. Once wampum had been exchanged between two or more tribes, they were allies who supported each other in danger and adversity.

The whites had their own ideas, however, and once they got it firmly fixed in their minds that wampum was a token of value and a medium of exchange, they began manufacturing the beads for their own use. At one time wampum was the accepted currency in most of the northern colonies, and the beads were being turned out on lathes, by the barrelful, especially at a factory in New Jersey. The original meaning of wampum exchange was totally lost. The beads became so common that they finally lost their worth as currency. In time, all beads made or worn by Indians were referred to as "wampum."

Among the northeastern stay-at-homes wampum kept its old meaning and its old value. Strands and belts of the beads became family and tribal heirlooms, treasured and handed down from generation to generation, with the stories of original owners and recipients still remembered and repeated.

Gladys Tantaquidgeon, a Mohegan girl, was practically adopted by anthropologist Frank Speck, and because of his influence and training she was graduated from the University of Pennsylvania with a degree in anthropology of her own. Her objectivity and frankness have provided us with accounts—too few and too scattered, unfortunately—of what life was like for a coastal Indian girl, growing up in the twentieth century in her conservative grandmother's home. There she learned to speak Mohegan, an Algonquian language, learned many of the old-style women's crafts, and was taught the nature and uses of many wild plants. It is through such rare people that what knowledge we have of the lives of northeastern Indians has been preserved.

Treaties, treaties, and more treaties. Some tribes of the Iroquoian Confederacy were removed to Indian Territory (now northeastern Oklahoma). Others were settled on reservations whittled from their own old lands in northern New York State.

The Delaware, Miami, Piankashaw, and Wea were first removed to Ohio, then to Kansas, and finally to a part of Indian Territory, where they were wedged between the Seneca and Wyandot and the Cherokee. There they formed an Algonquian-speaking island, and from there some Delaware shifted in the early nineteenth century to western Oklahoma, where they formed another isolated group, tucked in between the Kiowa and the Caddoans. And still white men wrote the treaties, and still Indian "leaders" were induced to touch the pen, and still more tribes were moved westward.

Even the vast Great Lakes region was becoming overcrowded. The native Chippewa and Santee Sioux were pushed aside by bands of Sauk and Fox, Kickapoo, Potawatomi, and Iowa. Southward, along the Ohio River, the Shawnee formed another Algonquian passageway between their northern relatives and the Creek. The position of the Shawnee has always been somewhat ambiguous. They are culturally more southern than any other Algonkians, and have always been associated with certain Creek and Cherokee bands. At the same time, their linguistic and tribal identity has remained clear. More than any other tribe, the Shawnee linked the Indians of the northeast with those of the southeast.

It was the presence of these cultural buffers that made possible the reservation of native culture in the heart of the country when it had long since vanished from its original location.

The culture of the Great Lakes tribes became a blend of coastal, woodland, and inland traits. A little pottery persisted into the early nineteenth century, but early reliance on trade goods and their replacement of articles of native manufacture restricted both pottery making and wood carving. Beadwork replaced porcupine-quill and moosehair embroidery, as did ribbon appliqué.

Most distinctive was the rise of the Medicine Lodge, or Mediwiwin, religion, which spread from tribe to tribe around the Lakes.

The teaching of the Medicine Lodge was the oneness of

man and nature. It was believed that a great and good spirit, the Manitou, had sent otters from the waters to be his messengers to the people, to teach them, and to encourage them.

Otter skins played an important part in Medicine Lodge ceremonialism. Both men and women participated in the ceremony, which took place in a special shelter. The two sides of the shelter, north and south, were occupied by two rows of worshipers. Each larger group was divided into smaller ones, and each subgroup had its own leaders and its own songs and prayers. The groups alternated in singing, each singer accompanying himself with a turtle-shell rattle.

At intervals during the ceremony, participants who had passed through the rising stages of initiation danced. They shook their otter skins at other members of the society and magically "shot" the others with cowrie shells. The shells were believed to enter the worshipers' bodies, and those who were shot fell unconscious or went into a trance state. Later the shells were vomited up and displayed in the "shooters' " hands, so that everyone could know their great power.

Water, and the water animals such as otters, turtles, and shellfish, were the bringers of good strength. Red and green ribbons were attached to the elaborately decorated otter skins; green representing the water and its power for good; red symbolizing war, blood, and destructiveness. The two had to be kept in balance in order for life to be good.

Opposed to the Manitou was an evil spirit, Gitchi Manitou, whose presence throughout life was symbolized by the red ribbons. In some instances the Manitou was equated with Jesus Christ, and the Gitchi Manitou was said to be Jesus' younger brother, or the devil. In other cases, the two retained their original characters without equation with outside religion.

Primarily, the Mediwiwin was a healing cult, and as time passed, the emphasis on its healing qualities came to overshadow the other powers for good implicit in the religion. One of the writers of this book was able to collect a unit group of Mediwiwin songs and the otter skins to which they "belonged" in Oklahoma in recent years. The religion is still actively practiced in some other places.

18

The Midlands

The southern Siouan occupied the Mississippi Valley; the northern Siouan territory stretched upstream along the Missouri and its tributaries. The word Siouan suggests that these people all spoke one language, or at least dialects of one language. That is not strictly true; their languages were technically related but were not mutually intelligible. Their cultures varied widely; the northern and western Dakota and Lakota bands must be considered a part of the true Plains culture, while the southern and eastern Dhegiha were linked culturally to the Lakes and river groups of Algonkians.

We are particularly concerned at the moment with the Dhegiha, and specifically with the Osage, who held the balance of power between the French and Spanish, and then between the Spanish and the United States, from the middle of the sixteenth century until the first quarter of the nineteenth.

Allied with the Osage were the Quapaw, the Ponca, the Kaw, the Oto, and, to a lesser extent, the Iowa. These people did speak mutually intelligible languages, and their cultures were similar.

All were semihorticultural, semihunting peoples. When gardens had been planted and the young plants had begun to grow, the women rolled up the mat coverings of their vaulted rectangular dwellings and piled the mats on top of the frames. Caches of dried meat and of the previous year's crops were made in the form of bundles hung from the limbs of trees. Fires were extinguished, and only a few of the oldest and most disabled persons were left in the village to guard the stores. Every able-bodied man and woman set out on the summer hunt. At this time they lived, Plains fashion, in small skin-covered tipis.

When the hunters returned, the village was practically rebuilt. New rushes were gathered and new mats were plaited, although the summer shelters generally were brush arbors or rectangular frames covered with slabs of elm bark. All dwellings, at whatever season of the year, faced eastward.

In the autumn the whole process was repeated. The returning village moved into the mat houses for the winter. Traders for furs might visit the village at any time in the year, although early summer, when the winter pelts were piled high and the summer hunt had not yet begun, was the preferred time. In return for beaver and otter pelts, dressed buffalo and deer skins, and dried meat, the traders brought the inevitable brass kettles, rum or brandy, arms and ammunition, red and blue woolen cloth named for the town of Stroud, England, where it was loomed, English calicoes and muslins, French ribbons, bolts of silk, laces, and Venetian glass beads. These beads were smaller, finer, and more regular in size and shape than the pony beads of the English traders. Since the French traders traveled by canoe, they could carry heavier and more bulky wares than could the pack traders.

Knives, adzes, axes, and tomahawks were also carried by the traders. This is probably an appropriate time and place to mention that the tomahawk, as we know it, was of European invention and manufacture. Certain eastern tribes had the customs of smoking a peace pipe and burying a hatchet when they declared peace, and of digging up the hatchet when they renewed hostilities.

It took European perceptiveness and ingenuity to see that the two functions could be combined in a single article. The combined pipe-weapon was then cast in iron or bronze, given as sharp an edge as it would take, and shipped overseas for trade to the simple savages. Since the stem of a pipe—its calumet—was the sacred part of the pipe to the Indians, the fact that the hatchet function of the tomahawk required a straight, heavy, solid stem was not important. Often a haft and a pipestem were used interchangeably. The great native weapon from the Great Lakes southward was the war club, often angled in shape, like a gunstock, with a stone or metal knife blade secured in the outward bend of the angle.

Strouding, ribbon, and scissors had at least as profound an effect on dress as firearms, ammunition, and metal knives and axes had on hunting and fighting. In the old pretrade days women's dress, in particular, had consisted of a wraparound skirt and a loose blouse of deerskin, sometimes ornamented with porcupine-quill embroidery. Now the same garments could be cut from cloth and decorated with ribbons or beads. Tribally distinctive styles of ribbon appliqué and of sewn beadwork soon developed, based on the decorative styles used in quillwork, and they are still made today, from the Great Lakes southward into Oklahoma.

Plaited belts, mats, garters, and bags were still made after the introduction of European fabrics to the Mississippi Valley but, with the exception of mats and storage bags, were more and more used for ceremonial purposes only. A distinctive feature of Osage belts was a border an inch or so wide into which were plaited strings of white pony beads.

It would take another volume twice the size of this one to describe the styles of dress, the minute and subtle difference in the making of belts, garters, and hair ribbons, the intricacies of beadwork and ribbon appliqué, that developed from the Great Lakes southward. This is neither the time nor the place for such descriptions. The point at present is that by the beginning of the eighteenth century these inland tribes were largely dependent on the traders for articles of everyday use and wear. Therefore it was important to these Indians to continue good trade relations, even to the extent of supporting one European nation in its struggles with another.

The signing of the Treaty of Paris in 1763 put an end to France's colonial empire in the New World, and the results were drastically felt in the northeast. In the Mississippi Valley, where French territory passed in theory to a weak and largely disinterested Spain, the effect was less disturbing.

Here the French traders continued their operations almost undisturbed. St. Louis and New Orleans, the two greatest river ports and trading centers, were French cities, founded and still largely occupied by Frenchmen. Cape Girardeau, St. Genevieve, Baton Rouge—the list of French names stretched for thousands of miles along the river.

The control of the trade of this vast area was largely in the hands of the Chouteau family, which was based in St. Louis. They employed the voyageurs who brought in skins and took out European goods. There were other great families, to be sure, but the Chouteaus were supreme.

Moreover, the Chouteaus carried on a generations-long love affair with the Osage tribe. Time and again one reads their references to "the mighty Osage," "the great Osage," "*les Osage suprêmes.*" Although Auguste Chouteau, founder of St. Louis and head of the clan, never married, both his brothers and some of his nephews had Osage wives.

Since the jumping-off point for the Rocky Mountains and the Great Plains was St. Louis, Chouteau influence included every traveler, or party of travelers, who had to be outfitted for the overland journey. And since they were civilized and hospitable men, the Chouteau influence touched such intellectual travelers as Washington Irving, Victor Tixier, and even Harriet Martineau. It undoubtedly influenced the writings of these persons, with the result that we have today more detailed descriptions of late-eighteenth-century and early-nineteenth-century Osage life than that of the cognate tribes.

The principal rival of the Chouteaus for the southern fur trade was Manual Lisa, of Spanish descent, who also had his headquarters in St. Louis for a time, and was briefly a partner in the Chouteau firm.

Lisa joined with the Spanish viceroy in plans to link the Spanish colonies of New Mexico and Louisiana and to take over the French trade on either side of the river. Lisa's part in this exploit is still cloudy and uncertain. Was he mainly interested in self-aggrandizement, or was he truly a loyal subject of Spain? Some authorities take one view and some another.

While the power struggle continued between the Chouteau family and Lisa, the United States began to awaken to the possibilities of the west as a dumping ground for surplus Indians. The Old Settlers of the Cherokee Nation had taken up land in what is now Arkansas, between the White and St. Francis rivers. This had displaced the native Quapaw, and driven that tribe westward into the territory of their Osage relatives. The Osage were willing to accommodate a few Quapaw from time to time, but a whole tribe at once was too much of a good thing. The Osage joined with the Quapaw against the Cherokee, and an undeclared war began.

The European nations continued trading lands among themselves. Spain sold Louisiana—which extended to the Pacific Ocean on the west and an undefined boundary on the north—back to France. Napoleon resold this territory to the United States. He needed guns, not real estate. James Monroe manipulated the Louisiana Purchase in Paris, and Thomas Jefferson in Washington took a deep breath and set about the task of persuading an impoverished Congress to pay for the property the ambassador had bought.

This is oversimplification, of course, as much of this book must of necessity be. Treaty followed treaty, and the involved minuet of diplomacy consumed months and years in time. Meanwhile, the Chouteaus succeeded in removing Lisa from the Mississippi Valley and west to New Mexico, and they and the Osage continued in control of the Mississippi.

Fifteen million dollars bought an unknown, unmapped, unexplored stretch of territory that extended the United States from ocean to ocean. It was necessary, to Jefferson's scientific mind, to find out just what the area included, and where it began and ended. England, basing her claim on Drake's explorations, denied the United States the California coast. Spain, by right of conquest and long occupancy, claimed Texas, New Mexico, Arizona, California, "and whatever lands are thereto adjacent." England again, by right of conquest of France, claimed the country to the north, from the Atlantic, around Hudson Bay and north again to the Arctic Circle, while Russia, thanks to Nicholas I, advanced a demand to be recognized as the owner of Alaska and British Columbia.

Because Louisiana had been purchased from France, the first exploring party set out to examine the country north of the Mississippi-Missouri confluence, with the intention of reaching the Pacific Ocean overland if such a tremendous task could be accomplished.

Captains Meriwether Lewis, commanding, and William Clark, second in command, traveled by keelboat down the Ohio and Mississippi, taking with them a small detachment of troops and their personal servants. The Congressional appropriation which financed the expedition had been made as secretly as possible, so that the interested European nations should not learn of its departure until it was under way.

Like everyone else, Lewis and Clark outfitted in St.

Louis at "the establishment of Mr. C." and, like everyone else, enjoyed his hospitality.

They engaged some of his voyageurs and *coureurs du bois* as guides, among them one Touissaint Charbonneau, married to an Indian girl whom Clark, in despair at pronouncing or spelling her own name, always called Janie. She had been born a Snake, or Shoshoni, Indian, captured as a child by the "Minatarees" of the upper Missouri, and discovered among the latter group by Charbonneau on one of his journeys west. She was to guide the expedition from the upper Missouri villages to the Rocky Mountains and the hunting lands of her own people. She was to become, under her Shoshoni name of Sacajawea, one of the three or four American Indian women whose names are known to all of us.

The expedition left St. Louis in the spring of 1804 and traveled upriver by boat as far as was feasible. From the villages of the Mandan and Hidatsa, Lewis and Clark struck overland, toiling through the foothills, to the uplands where the Shoshoni lived. From there on, they were without guides, for the country was strange to Janie, and they had to plot their course by compass—until the compass got lost in a stream crossing and they were forced to depend on the stars for guidance.

The expedition lived off the country, for the most part. The men hunted and fished, and Janie showed them what wild plants could be safely gathered and eaten. At one time Clark fell into a flooding river, and Janie helped to get him out. Another time she fell sick with what, from the description, must have been pneumonia, and Clark nursed her back to health. The father-daughter relationship between the two was undoubtedly one factor that carried them, at last, to the Pacific.

For they reached it, in November, 1805, at the mouth of the Columbia. For the first time on record non-Indian Americans had crossed the continent, seen what there was to be seen, and recorded what they saw and did; and, with 4,000 toilsome miles ahead of them, they braced themselves for the return journey.

Today the trip from Washington, D.C., to Portland, Oregon, consumes four hours' flying time.

At St. Louis, in September, 1806, the party regained the hospitality of Mr. C. On the return trip the two leaders had separated. Clark made a side expedition to the Yellowstone River and Lewis to the Marias River. They had rejoined forces for the last leg of the journey on the upper Missouri.

This was a well-recorded expedition, and it set a model, in that sense, for future explorers. Not only did each of the leaders keep a detailed journal; several of the enlisted men in the company did also. Even though one set of documents had been lost with the compass, the others remained, and it is possible today to reconstruct the whole journey, day by day and mile by mile, from these meticulously kept and atrociously spelled records.

From St. Louis, Lewis started east, while Clark remained to wind up the business details. Charbonneau abandoned his wife and child, to return to trapping on the upper Missouri. Janie herself simply disappeared. Some say she died of a broken heart, others that she found her way back to Shoshoni country, and there is a persistent legend to the effect that she and her little boy eventually traveled southwest, to the country of the Shoshoni-speaking Comanche, where she found shelter and hospitality, and where she eventually died. No one knows for sure, the Comanche say.

Only one man of the Lewis and Clark expedition died on the way, and only one deserted. These facts in themselves speak for the morale, courage, and determination of the whole party. The journey was a tremendous feat of physical endurance, but Lewis and Clark and their party had not climbed mountains "just because they were there." They had established a new skill, that of scientific exploration for a known reason, and all the men who came after them were in their debt for that.

Clark lived out his life in St. Louis. He succeeded Auguste Pierre Chouteau, a civilian, as Indian agent of the United States for the Northwest Territories, for Indian administration then came under the War Department. In time, Clark became governor of Missouri Territory. His name is inextricably woven with the events of the first half of the nineteenth century throughout the area.

Lewis' personal effect on history was briefer. In 1809, on a trip from St. Louis to Washington, he died suddenly —he was probably murdered—when he stopped overnight at a tavern near Nashville, Tennessee. All the circumstances surrounding his death have never been told, and the question of murder or not murder has never been resolved.

All in all, the Lewis and Clark expedition was a fruitful one. It showed that the inland part of the continent was inhabited, and by whom. It suggested trade routes, overland and by water. It revealed the potentials of the northern half of a subcontinent. And it came at a time when such potentials were badly needed by the new nation that was expanding inland from the Atlantic coast. New population pressure was building from the east.

19

Over the Waters

EUROPE WAS SEETHING AT THE BEGINNING OF THE NINE-teenth century. The French peasants, the best-fed, best-educated, and best-led of the masses, had risen in revolution. The educated middle class—the bourgeoisie—came forward, to build a republic on the ruins of a monarchy, and were in their turn beaten down by a sprig of poverty-stricken Italian nobility. The displaced, aristocrats and bourgeois alike, fled in clusters to England, and some, like the Abbé Talleyrand, even made their way for a time to the New World.

England, meanwhile, had troubles of its own. The king was mad. His son, the regent, was extravagant, diseased, and indifferent to any part of government except the gathering in of moneys. Church and parliament were both corrupt, and while there were men who struggled to clean out each, they were still a long way from reaching success.

Into this international situation, already bad enough, two mechanical inventions were hurled. One was the spinning jenny, or mechanical spinning wheel. The other was the steam engine, which could be applied not only to transportation but to weaving. A whole stratum of prosperous skilled crafts workers suddenly found themselves unemployed and, unless they learned new trades, without hope of future employment.

Children could be put to work in the coal mines that stoked the steam engines, but grown men, who demanded a living wage, had a hard time finding jobs. So, little by little, at first a few at a time and then in a rising flood, indentured or contracted laborers crossed the ocean.

There was need and demand for skilled laborers in the east. Cities were rising, and with them industries were growing. Massachusetts and Connecticut, in particular, were poor in agricultural resources but rich in water-power. Pennsylvania was developing its industries, as was New York. The immigrants were welcome in the east and found work with little difficulty.

At the same time, these newcomers had to be fed, and city workers can do little about feeding themselves from the soil. Agriculture expanded with industry, and the fertile valleys from Pennsylvania westward became, for the time, the breadbasket of the world.

Now there could no longer be romantic nonsense about the red children of nature and their simple hunting life. The hunting lands were needed to put to the plow, or for grazing sheep and cattle. *Niles Weekly Register*, published in London, described the Mississippi Valley as "the Flanders of America" and predicted that land around St. Louis would soon be worth $200 an acre. The newsletter urged English emigrants to set out for this promised—if malarial—land while they could still purchase good farms at $2 an acre.

They had nothing to lose and very much to gain. The raw, newly built factories were sprawling across lands that had once been farm and pasture. Hopelessness lay behind the emigrants, for crops had failed for three years, but there might be hope ahead. Skilled farmers followed the traders, and Indian lands were once again compressed.

The Indians were beginning to feel the pressure, and to resent it. Delegation after delegation visited Governor Clark and aired its grievances. If they must live among white men—or with white men among them—and if the game and therefore their means of livelihood were taken from them, said the Osage, the Quapaw, the Ponca, and the Kaw, at least let them be given the equipment to live like white men. Their treaties had promised protection of their lands, and with it schools, missionaries, farmers, millwrights, wheelwrights, and other skilled workmen. Where were all these teachers of white life when the Indians needed them?

As it became evident that the Indians could not meet the oncoming competition, they began to move westward. In the century between 1750 and 1850 the writers have mapped the westward movement of the Osage alone—one hundred miles every ten years, from the Mississippi to the headwaters of the Candian, in western Kansas.

As the southern Siouan tribes moved westward, two things happened. The Indians lost many of the material traits which had linked them to the Great Lakes tribes, and they acquired many Plains Indian traits. From being "riverine" peoples they became equestrian ones. They used tipis for two reasons: there were no rushes to make mats, and there were buffalo to provide skins for shelter, clothing, and other needs.

For a time the Osage and Quapaw hoped that they could find shelter in the Arkansas woods. But there were those strange people, the Cherokee, who spoke an outlandish tongue, lived in houses and farmed like white men, and were friends with Mrs. P. Lovely, the widow of the trader who ran the post known as Lovely's Purchase. The Cherokee said they had bought this land from the United States. It seemed strange that both parties to the transaction should have ignored the Osage and Quapaw.

Pierre Chouteau, in an effort to relieve the growing tension, induced Claremont's band of Osage to move with him to the upper fork of the Verdigris River and there establish a new trading and hunter center, which was later to be known as Claremore, Oklahoma. Unfortunately, this location, too, soon proved to be on Cherokee-claimed land, and the Osage had to move on again.

In the 1820's Mexico gained its independence from Spain. Spanish trading regulations had been stringent; only traders from Mexico or Spain could cross the Rio Grande, the boundary between the states of Durango and Chihuahua on one side of the river and the Mexican Territory of New Mexico on the other. Now, traders from other nations, especially from the United States, were invited into New Mexico, to trade at Sante Fe and Taos.

Crossing the Plains was hazardous. Kiowa and Comanche in the southern Plains; Cheyenne and Arapaho in the central Plains, and Dakota to the north—all were feeling the encroachment of the newcomers. Many of the Missouri traders, particularly, employed Pawnee guides, and the Pawnee were thoroughly unpopular with everyone else. The reasons are numerous; the Pawnee practiced an annual sacrifice of a captive woman; they were aggressive Caddoans, which seemed to the other tribes a contradiction of terms, and for two centuries they had been active slave traders with the Spaniards and the French. This had led to the not surprising consequence that when other tribes captured Pawnee, they in turn went into the slave-dealing business, with the result that a synonym for "slave" became Pawnee, from New Orleans to St. Louis.

Any party of traders who appeared on the Plains with Pawnee guides took its risks and had to be prepared to suffer the consequences. This was an added hazard, but the Plains were as trackless as a desert, for all the tall and short grass that covered them. Without landmarks and without guides it was almost impossible to steer safely from water to water.

So again it was trade that linked two parts of the continent. Trade with the descendants of the Spanish colonists at first; later, trade with the Kiowa and Comanche who, like everybody else, had depended on Mexican traders who called themselves *Comancheros* as a boast of their daring in venturing into Comanche lands.

Again eastern industry expanded, following the rivers as all peoples had. Pittsburgh became a shipbuilding center, and soon other industries developed there. The Du Pont family set up their powder mill at Wilmington, Delaware, and carried on regular correspondence, in both French and English, with the Chouteau family in St. Louis. One wonders what those two autocrats, Auguste Chouteau and the first Eleuthère Irénée Du Pont, would have had to say to each other, and in what language they would have said it, had they met in person.

The demand for armaments increased after the turn of the nineteenth century. Beaver-plush hats for men had gone out of style and had been replaced by silk-plush hats made from a fabric milled at Lyons, France. Now it was the leather resources of the west that must be developed; there was no stronger or longer-wearing leather than that made from buffalo hide. If Indian-tanned hides were not available, the cobblers of Boston and Hartford could dress flint hides, or rawhides, by European processes, as could the glove makers of Philadelphia and some of the southern cities. It was generally agreed, however, that Indian-tanned buckskins, when they were available, made the best and finest gloves.

So industry spread, and trade went up and down the rivers, or trade goods were hauled overland by mule or ox-trains. And steadily, inexorably, the Indian country was invaded and the Indians were pushed aside. Just as inexorably, the Indians returned to the sources of trade goods, for now they were dependent on the white men for most of the luxuries and many of the necessities of life. Commerce and the steamboat—and soon the steamcars—were shrinking the distance between the oceans and making possible all the great changes that kept coming . . . coming . . . coming . . .

Part Three

Transition

20

The Edge of the World

JUST AS CHANGE HAD STRUCK THE MISSISSIPPI VALLEY, so it moved westward, as the Indians moved, into the Great Plains. Here intertribal lines had been as sharply drawn as anywhere on the continent, since the horses had come to change the Indian world.

To the south, the Comanche ranged from the Sierra Madre in northern Mexico to the southern slopes of the Wichita Mountains in southwestern Oklahoma, and west into the Staked Plains of the Oklahoma and Texas Panhandles. North of them, the Kiowa hunted from the northern slopes of the Wichitas to the Arkansas River headwaters, in western Kansas. Arapaho, Ute, and Shoshoni occupied Colorado, from east to west, and their territory extended north into that of the Cheyenne in Wyoming and Montana. North and east of the Cheyenne the many northern Siouan divisions took over, while north again were the Gros Ventre, the Mandan and Hidatsa, and the various Blackfoot units. Over this wide stretch of country two main buffalo herds ranged, one northern and one southern, each shifting as the grazing changed with the seasons. Half the continent was buffalo country.

The first incursion of the eastern tribes into the true Plains must have come before 1800, for the Pawnee were recognized enemies of the other groups by that date. In 1832 a band of Osage attacked a Kiowa hunting camp in the Wichitas while the men were away, cut off the heads of women and children, and left them bubbling over their cooking fires for the husbands to find on their return. In due course the husbands returned, found one of the characteristically Osage "gunstock" clubs that had been dropped, and set out for revenge.

The constant menace of the tribes east of the Cross Timbers brought about unions and coalitions in the Plains. The Kiowa, Kiowa Apache, and Lipan joined hands with their traditional enemies, the Comanche, to resist the new danger. Cheyenne and Arapaho united so strongly that they became officially known as "the Cheyenne-Arapaho tribe," and made joint peace with the more southern tribes. The Sioux drew closer together, so that whereas once it had been necessary to speak of each group by its individual name, it was now possible for government officials to refer to "the Sioux tribe."

Until 1849, when the Department of the Interior was established by act of Congress and the Bureau of Indian Affairs made part of it, all Indians were under military jurisdiction. Between wars troops were few and underpaid; during warfare they were needed elsewhere.

Until 1846, the Comanche and Kiowa in particular largely controlled commerce across the southern Plains from Missouri to Santa Fe. The Santa Fe Trail, which began at Independence, Missouri, was wide and well defined, and traders' wagons—known as prairie schooners, were shiplike visible, as they rolled across the ocean of grass. It was an easy matter to swoop down on them, surround the wagons, and either demand blackmail in the form of trade goods or, if this was refused, simply eliminate wagons and wagoners, the goods having been removed in preparation for the destruction of the wagons.

The Kiowa, like some other Plains tribes, had the habit of keeping a year count, or calendar, a series of pictographs drawn spirally on buckskin, representing the principal events of each season. The Kiowa counted two years to our one—a summer year and a winter year. In the calendars the summers were represented by a drawing of a Sun Dance lodge; in the winter barren trees were drawn. Each summer or winter year was named for the event the older men considered most significant. For instance, 1832 was THE YEAR THE OSAGE CUT OFF THEIR HEADS, while 1833 was THE YEAR THE STARS FELL—the famous meteor shower that was observed everywhere in North America.

Tribes other than the Kiowa kept year counts, and from the pictographic drawings which illustrated the records an art style developed, amazingly homogeneous for the whole Plains area. Probably the brief length of time consumed by the history of the Plains tribes as such accounts for the similarity of drawings from tribe to tribe; such great similarity, in fact, that for many years any art executed by Indians of any culture area had to follow the two-dimensional style of the mid-nineteenth-century Plains to be considered "Indian."

There are differences from tribe to tribe, as one would expect. The Ming-like horses drawn by the Cheyenne could never be confused with the hook-hoofed creatures the Crow and the Dakota tribes liked to depict, any more than they could be with the blockily realistic beasts the Kiowa portrayed.

The same art forms, naturalistic and historic, decorated men's robes, and the tipis in which the men held their social or ceremonial gatherings, all of which portrayed in detail the wearer's or owner's accomplishments. A man's shield often was similarly decorated, either with a picture of one of his battles or with his power symbol.

In their rare moments of leisure, the Plains Indian women visited each other, entertaining and being entertained. Their main function was listening, for a man could be in only one place at one time, while his wives could drift from one to another of several places. It is notable even today that a Plains Indian tribal council seldom makes or announces a decision the first day that it meets. Husbands go home to talk things over with their wives before finally declaring themselves.

Because most Plains ethnology—certainly most early ethnology—was written by men who interviewed other men, our clearest accounts of Plains life were concerned with men's lives: with the vision quest, participation in war parties, weapon making, and the like. Women and their occupations were largely overlooked until the twentieth century.

A distinction must be made, throughout the Plains, between the "war chiefs" and the "peace chiefs." Any man who felt himself strong enough and popular enough to do so could head a war party. Some men were so successful in raiding and in capturing horses and women that they had the status successful generals have among us today. But chiefs' status did not mean that they could make peace for a whole tribe, or that they could in any way commit their people to a treaty or an agreement.

Such commitments were the province of the councils of peace chiefs. These were usually older men, although young men of recognized statesmanship and diplomacy were sometimes admitted to the peace chiefs' councils. The young men only listened, as part of their training for the future.

The tightness of organization of the peace chiefs' councils varied, from the utter informality of the Kiowa and Comanche, through the band organization of most of the Siouans, to the strict formality of the Council of the Forty and Four, of the Cheyenne. One Arapaho was always included among the four leading Cheyenne chiefs, and the Arapaho returned the courtesy. As was once said, "These offices weren't exactly hereditary. They just kind of come down in the same families."

One thing that must always be kept in mind in discussing intratribal, intertribal, and extratribal relations is that nowhere in Indian thinking did our concept of majority rule exist. There was unanimity or there was nothing.

This fact is especially important to remember in the treaty period of which we are writing. Because one man touched the pen, the representatives of the United States government believed an entire tribe was committed to the agreement. That simply was not true. Nobody was committed but the person who actually scratched the paper with the pen.

The pattern of disruption that had removed the southeastern tribes to new lands was repeated in the Plains. There were variations on the main theme, of course. In some tribes, where bands were scattered over a wide area and the chiefs saw each other formally only once a year, the signature of a single band leader was held binding on all his peers. It actually was not binding until all the others formally agreed to sign. There had to be unanimity.

On certain occasions, such as the signing of a treaty at Medicine Lodge, Kansas in 1871—which was not ratified by the Senate until 1872—notice was sent to many tribes to meet at one place at one time, but the message never seemed to reach the leaders of the hostile bands until the meeting was finished and over. After the placators had signed, the hostiles rallied in protest.

The discovery of gold in California had a profound effect on the Plains Indians. Heretofore, the Cross Timbers had been called "impenetrable" and let go at that. Now it was desirable to find a way across the continent to the goldfields without making the long journey around Cape Horn, the shorter but equally unpleasant one across the Isthmus of Panama, or the risky trip overland through the Rockies, where whole parties, snowed in, died of starvation or resorted to cannibalism. The miners did not have a Janie to show them the way.

In 1850 Colonel Randolph B. Marcy set out to find a way along the river, through the Timbers, and across the plains to California. He had the first prolonged encounters of white troops with the Kiowa, Comanche, and southern Athabascans since the first dragoon expedition left Cantonment Gibson in 1832. Troops other than Marcy's were exploring the northern plains.

All field officers agreed that a chain of frontier garrison posts was needed, extending from Texas north to the Canadian border, and from St. Louis to the west coast. Troops were to be stationed at St. Louis and Sante Fe, and the old Spanish presidio at San Francisco was to be reactivated for the United States Army.

The coming, first of the miners, then of the soldiers, and finally of the settlers, whether cattlemen or farmers, marked the end of the true Plains culture. A wave of cultural disintegration spread across the area. Sexual mores became less strict—the Plains tribes were undergoing the same exposure to outside "husbands" that had already changed the character of the eastern tribes.

In the north central Plains, especially among the Sioux, one resistance feature was to dance all night so that, presumably, the troops should have as little rest as possible. These "Forty-Nine" dances, as they have come to be called, are a fascinating feature of intertribal Indian culture today.

Forty-Nine dances always take place late at night, usually following a ceremonial or social dance. Linked couples join hands, shuffling around a cluster of drummers, and pressing closer and closer together in a tightening spiral. As the night wears on, one couple after another disappears into the shielding night, and nine months later the next crop of "Forty-Nine babies" appears to distress missionaries and administrators.

Forty-Nine songs are a curious compound of English and native words, and of the nonsense syllables into which the latter are transposed by speakers of other languages:

I don't care if you've been married fifty times,
I love you, darling.
I don't care if you have fifteen children,
I'll get you yet,
Yah yah yah yah.

Another favorite is:

When the dance is over, sweetheart,
I will take you home
In my one-eyed Ford.

And still another Forty-Nine song goes:

They say you won't love me,
If I drink whiskey.
Sweet whiskey, I love you,
I'll drink you till I die.

When one of the authors of this book began her fieldwork, in the early 1930's, the country was going through the same kind of upheaval it had experienced in the middle nineteenth century. At that time Forty-Nine dances still went on in secluded clearings, but it was not considered "nice" to attend them. The other writer, on the other hand, beginning fieldwork in the 1950's, was invited and even urged by her Indian friends to attend and take part in Forty-Nine dances, so much had times changed in two decades.

Forty-Nine dancing, however, was only one development of resistance to Army influence. Another, and more exciting, method of the 1850's was to steal horses from an enemy tribe, cull the herd, and sell the rejects to the troops. This had the double advantage of immobilizing one enemy and of slowing down the other. Twenty years later, in 1870, Colonel George Custer reported to Washington that the Indians were "better mounted, better armed, and had the added advantage of their women to bring up spare horses as they were needed, so that the braves went always freshly mounted, while our horses were jaded from travel."

Not only arms came into the frontier posts. The sutlers—or traders—who traveled with the troops and supplied them with tobacco, whiskey, etc., soon began to stock items for the Indian trade. It was fair enough to trade in the traditional manner: pelts, horses, and so on, but a good deal less expensive to waylay the wagon trains, especially those paymasters' trains which brought shiny metal disks to the posts, and thereby obtain the trade goods without trading. How many bull whippers and mule skinners laid their bones beside the trails to frontier garrisons can never be known.

The outbreak of the Civil War meant withdrawal, at first slow, but rapidly increasing in speed, of soldiers from the western frontier. For a large part of the conflict, from 1862 to 1865, the United States depended on the loyal Lighthorsemen of the Five Civilized Tribes to hold the southwestern frontier against the marauders who were taking over one post after another. Better frontier guards never rode. To the Cherokee and their allies, the Plains Indians were not "red brothers" but "hostiles," to be eliminated ruthlessly.

From 1860 to 1865 Plains culture underwent a recrudescence. It rose to new heights and flourished as never before. From Kansas north, settlers who lacked the protection of the Lighthorsemen banded together in local bodies of militia, or fled before the advancing storm. Reservation boundaries were forgotten or ignored, and "the finest light cavalry of the world" ruled its own roost once more.

Eighteen sixty-six saw the reactivation of the old frontier posts and the establishment of new ones. Many officers and men who had seen service during the war and felt uprooted and dissatisfied in civilian life requested frontier posts. Irish immigrants who had fled from the potato famine of the 1840's; German hussars who were tired of waiting out peacetimes at home and had enlisted with the Union as mercenaries; English younger sons who saw an opportunity for land as well as for excitement and adventure among the "redmen"; Negro Freedmen and young men who knew no trade but soldiering—these made up the military on the Plains. Food was poor, and clothing and equipment worse, but there was excitement and adventure and $30 at the end of each month, and it was better than nothing, after all.

So there were men on either side with nothing to lose and everything to gain, confronting each other in the Plains from 1865 to 1876. The declared mission of the military was to confine the Indians to reservation areas where they had agreed by treaty to locate; the declared mission of the Indians was to disregard the treaties and do away with the troopers.

As permanent posts were established, and stone fortifications surrounded them, both officers and men began to bring their wives west, if they could afford it. There were also those ubiquitous hangers-on of army posts, the "laundresses," who fulfilled more than one function in a society where men outnumbered women a hundred to one.

And, as the net grew tighter and the Indians moved

nearer to the posts, for protection or material advantages, there began to be a new class among Plains Indian women. Heretofore, any woman who was in some degree promiscuous was known in her tribe as "crazy." Soon promiscuity was supporting many Plains Indian families, while the men of the family looked the other way—usually down.

For the railroads were a-building, and the buffalo were imposing traffic jams along the rails. The eastern builders hired ex-soldiers, scouts, or farmers who were handy with guns, and between 1870 and 1872 the buffalo were all but eliminated. Only a few ragged remnants of the once great herds remained, huddled in obscure box canyons. There the survivors were found, and eventually rescued, by conservationists.

The destruction of the buffalo left in its wake a total demoralization. Men's jobs were gone, and the men, untrained for any work but hunting, were left idle. The women, bracing themselves to the inevitable, were not idle. They had to learn to make do with jackrabbits, prairie dogs, wood mice, and such small deer as they could snare for themselves. They were reduced to eating wild birds, wild eggs, terrapins, and even fish. Dog was no longer a dish to be served only on ceremonial occasions. Horses and mules were the last sacrifices to family appetites, but with the range fenced or gone, why let the horses and mules starve to death? Kill them and cook them.

As wire fencing spread westward, and prairies became pastures, the walls closed in on the Plains people. Such horses as were left ate cottonwood bark as often as prairie hay. A people whose lives had rested on a single economic base were left hanging in midair, deprived of their principal source of food, shelter, utensils, clothing, and equipment.

It did not happen all at once, and it did not happen easily. Every river had its battlefield; every bluff at some time was the scene of a siege. Better armed and better mounted in the beginning, the Plains Indians gradually diminished in worldly goods, expended their ammunition, and ate the straggly horses that remained to them.

Count the battle honors of the Seventh Cavalry alone: Antelope Hills, Washita, Little Big Horn (which eliminated all the regiment but its marching song, "Garry Owen," and Major Miles Keogh's great horse, Comanche); Wounded Knee. Only one military honor could be in any sense considered a battle, and in that the Indians, fighting with a superior knowledge of the terrain, were clearly the victors.

Every battle had its chroniclers, for the railroads went west with the troops, the telegraph lines looped beside the rails, and newspaper reporters accompanied commands into the field. Mark Kellogg, who filed his reports with, among other papers, the New York *Herald*, died with Custer at the Little Big Horn. But not before he had sent off a series of dispatches which were widely read and created a folk hero out of a blundering egotist.

More to be admired were the Negro troops, most of them Freedmen, who made up the Ninth and Tenth Cavalry regiments and whose holding actions controlled the fire of battle that threatened to sweep across the Plains and blot out every living thing. The Indians feared the "black white men" who rode into battle with wild cries and swinging sabres much as the Indians did themselves. There was an exultation in fighting Buffalo Soldiers; here were men who were not afraid to die, only to retreat, and the Indians could understand them while they dreaded them. Fear, admiration, and acceptance were what the Negro horsemen found, and they left their blood mark in many Indian families.

There was no one cause for the abrupt termination of Plains Indian culture. Greed inevitably played its part. Ambition was another factor, on either side. Still another was the increasing industrialization of the northeast, together with the devastation left by war in the once agricultural south. There was need for new lands. Agriculture and cattle raising had to expand if factory workers were to be fed after 1865.

Another cause, undoubtedly, for the elimination of Indian cultures was the increased wave of European immigration which followed the Franco-Prussian War. There were many Alsatians and other Frenchmen who found German domination unacceptable. They were followed by Swiss, northern Europeans, and other trained workers. British subjects formed classes of their own; the Irish became laborers, the Scots businessmen and bankers, and the English proper cattle breeders or soldiers. In each case the migrants displaced native North Americans, who now had a century and a half of occupancy of the continent behind them and who followed the course their forefathers had taken, westward, along the frontier.

The Plains were not the only battlefield of this distressed decade. Chief Moses of the Salish, on the Columbia; Chief Joseph of the Nez Perce, in interior Idaho; Chief Schonchin of the Modoc—all fought the same battles as Crazy Horse, Sitting Bull, Sitting Bear, White Bear, Nokoni, and Quanah, and all as ineffectually. Eventually they had to give up.

Geronimo summed the matter up for everybody, finally.

"He wasn't a chief," observed a centenarian who had been his follower. "He wasn't much of a medicine man. But he was the best we had left, so we drafted him to volunteer to lead us."

And when Geronimo surrendered, after dodging in and out between the Chiricahuas and the Sierra Madre, he expressed himself succinctly to General George Crook.

"I'm not surrendering to you," the reluctant warrior said. "I'm surrendering to your pack mules."

In the southwest, where the Navaho were harassing would-be stockmen, the pattern of roundup and removal was repeated yet once again. Colonel Kit Carson led a body of local militia and a few seasoned troops against the Navaho. The Navaho took refuge in the red fastness of the Canyon de Chelly, in Arizona, and stood off their enemies as long as food and water lasted.

Then, and only then, the Navaho surrendered. Under Carson's prodding, in 1863, the People set off on their trail of tears—the Long March—from northern Arizona to Fort Sumner, in southeastern New Mexico, crossing the desert country on foot.

Fort Sumner, be it understood, was not a concentration camp but an experiment in "civilization" and progressive farming. The Navaho, whose farming had previously been confined to small patches of corn, beans, and squash in canyon bottoms, were to become large-scale farmers of garden truck on irrigated land. This would make them self-supporting and eliminate their need for the sheep that were ruining the northern range lands. The experiment failed for the reason most such experiments fail: the irrigation water was not available. Three years of drought, sickness, death, frustration, and sullen refusal to cooperate with any whites on any project ended the experiment.

The Navaho trudged homeward across the desert, in 1866, from the stinking huts of the Bosque Redondo to the clean air of the Canyon de Chelly. There, with sheep issued to them by the Bureau of Indian Affairs, they reestablished themselves as stockmen, to become, in later years, the most prosperous of all Indian tribes.

21

The Alleviators

ULYSSES S. GRANT WAS A MOST UNHAPPY MAN. THE FIRST of Nathaniel Hawthorne's "bullet-headed generals" to enter the White House as President after the Civil War was no fool. He had proved that the hard way.

But Grant was in a curious position. He was as innocent as the babe unborn in matters of policy, politics, and high finance. He was by nature gentle with the helpless, and, by virtue of the period in which he lived, a sentimentalist. So Grant was doubly vulnerable. He could be bullied by financiers who trade on the ignorance of a country storekeeper. And he could be preyed upon by those men of the cloth who appealed to his better nature and his moral judgments.

History has never given Grant his due. He had never really fought side by side with the men who now took over the western commands which had once been his. George Armstrong Custer he went on record as disliking and distrusting. The surviving general officers Grant really knew, trusted, and judged on the merits of courage and efficiency were Robert E. Lee, now deprived of his citizenship along with his inherited wealth; George Crook, "the soldiers' soldier" during and after the war; and Oliver O. Howard, one-armed veteran of the conflict, "the praying general," who left a string of post chapels and Sunday schools taught by officers' wives as he went up and down the west.

Howard seems to have been, on the record, a completely selfless human being. He performed his duties flawlessly. He knew where his men were and what they were doing at any given moment, and they knew the same about him. He hated injury and the taking of human lives. Howard was the natural choice for Grant to send out as intermediary between the warring Indians and the military.

Howard did what he could, somewhat hampered by the fact that a great many of the officers nominally under his command ridiculed him and his praying, and that his best support came from the non-Indian frontiersmen who begged that churches be built and clergy sent out to them.

Howard's final recommendation to Grant was to remove the Indians from the further conflicts inevitably induced by the "protection" of the military and to transfer the management of Indian affairs to a civilian body. He suggested the revival of the ancient and honorable Bureau of Indian Affairs, placing it under the Department of the Interior—then, as always, a catchall for miscellaneous government bureaus—and putting in it as personnel as many members of the Society of Friends as could be induced to turn westward. In case the Quakers ran out, there were always Episcopalians, Presbyterians, Methodists, and Baptists. Catholic priests were, by ordination, prohibited from participation in government affairs, and Catholics were not too popular with frontiersmen away from the early areas of French and Spanish influence, in any case.

So a new brand of hero faced the western tribes. There were men like the Quaker Thomas Battey, who singlehanded held Kiowa and Comanche back from fighting when, in 1871, the military tried to punish them for the depredations of the Modoc war—so far away that the southern plains tribes had never heard of the Modoc.

John D. Miles, another Quaker, took over the southern Cheyenne Agency at Darlington, not too far from Fort Reno, and tried unsuccessfully to prevent the return of Chief Dull Knife's band to Montana when Oklahoma heat and dust proved more than the northerners could bear. Miles had the able and respected assistance of John Seger, the agency blacksmith, who finally decided that most of the Cheyenne were not worth the trouble he was taking to teach them blacksmithing and removed a group of promising Arapaho, together with a few of the milder Cheyenne, to what is now Colony, Oklahoma. There Seger founded a school, a workshop, and a farm, and drilled what he could of agriculture into the heads of the stubborn horsemen.

The story is told of how Seger, trying to make farming as respected by the Indians as it was by his brother German Mennonites, called the able-bodied men together into council. A council demanded finery, and the Indians came in what they had salvaged of their best buckskin and feathers. Seger took the handles of the plow and, with a two-mule team, ran a straight furrow from one end of the field to the other. Then he called up the war-bonneted men who watched him and put the plow handles in the hands of each in turn. And, in turn, each Indian ran a wavering shallow line, that really could not be called a furrow at all, along the surface of the ground. At last one old man, who had carefully watched the others as Seger demonstrated again and again after each failure, took his turn. His furrow was as deep and straight as Seger's own. And the old man's wives, watching, threw back their heads and trilled the victory call, for this was, indeed, triumph over the white man's tools.

Finally, there was Pratt. Richard Henry Pratt had been a brevet general officer during the Civil War, and was retired to his former grade of lieutenant colonel after Antietam. He was a West Pointer who firmly believed in education as the means of salvation for mankind. It was his request to Grant that he be allowed to open a school for Negro troopers, and later for the children of Negro Freedmen, at Hampton, Virginia, that led to one of the greatest educational experiments of the nineteenth century. Pratt could see no reason why the educational methods that worked with Negroes could not be extended to Indians.

Pratt's first Indian students were adults. All of the captive Chiricahua and Mescalero who had fought under Geronimo, together with some recalcitrant Kiowa, Comanche, Cheyenne, Arapaho, and Sioux, were imprisoned in the old Spanish fortress of San Marco, renamed Fort Marion, at St. Augustine, Florida, in 1873. There the prisoners killed time by learning pidgin English and by making drawings of battles and of the main events of their lives—of all the existence they had lost and for which they yearned—on any kind of paper they could cadge from the officers or troopers stationed to guard them. It was a dull and wearying survival, even after the Indians learned that their captors would pay good money for the drawings and, in turn, exchange tobacco and sweets for the money. There were women and children among the prisoners, and into the stagnant situation Pratt stepped, determined to do what he could for these helpless ones.

Pratt was not cut from the same piece of cloth as Howard, but their texture was similar. He was not a praying general himself, but he admitted Quaker missionaries, and later Mennonites, to his command post and encouraged them to work with the captives. The result was that the Indians' English improved; they learned trades and, when they were finally released, returned to their tribes with skills that could be used at the Army posts or the towns that were beginning to grow up near them.

Fort Marion was hardly the place to confine people who were used to a higher altitude, drier air, and freedom of movement. The disease and death rates were high, especially those from tuberculosis and pulmonary pneumonia. Pratt asked that the school, at least, be moved to a healthier location, and in 1879 the Department of the Interior granted Pratt's petition and moved the school to the partially abandoned Carlisle Barracks in Pennsylvania. There it continued until it was closed in 1920.

The effect of the Carlisle School on American Indian life and history can hardly be measured. The first children to be enrolled there were outright hostages for the good behavior of their parents. Pratt had brought some of his older students and most of his teachers from Fort Marion, and this group formed a core of trained personnel in the new environment.

Discipline at Carlisle School was military. Students, both boys and girls, wore uniforms and learned military drill on the pre-Revolutionary parade ground of the old post. They lived in barracks, literally, but the barracks were clean, warm, and in good repair. Pratt and his men saw to that.

Every student spent so many hours a day in class; so many more in workshops, stables, kitchens and bakery, and sewing rooms. The school's farm and herd made it largely self-sustaining. Every language but English was forbidden, and students who spoke their own languages were punished with extra drill and work assignments.

Six months of each year the students spent outside the school, on the "outing system." They were assigned to families in the vicinity, preferably rural families, where they lived and worked as members of the household. A legend has grown up that all these families were Quaker, but as a matter of fact more were Mennonite. The months of hard work, the necessity as compared with the compulsion to speak English, and the observation of peaceful, orderly daily life had a great influence on the lives of the students who participated in the Carlisle plan.

There were tragedies, of course. Some children simply willed themselves to die rather than live away from home. Others, whose lives up to that time had been spent in what was at least a "permissive disciplinary" atmosphere, rebelled against military discipline and organization and ran away. Sometimes students froze or starved to death before they reached home.

But there were still others who accepted Carlisle for what Pratt intended it to be: a refuge from economic insecurity, an opportunity to learn to compete squarely with non-Indians, and a chance to observe ways of life that were different from their own. Carlisle's participation in outside community life extended to sports, especially football. Carlisle is said to have won its first football game when an overstuffed Kiowa fell on the ball, flattening it. He tucked it under his jersey, wallowed down the field, and triumphantly produced the crushed bladder on the other side of the goal line—a touchdown.

They may be legendary, but Carlisle had great teams and great athletes in fields of sport other than football. It's athletes, Jim Thorpe and Namoki among them, competed successfully in the Olympics. In fact, Thorpe, a Sauk, is known as the greatest American athlete of all times. Later, he organized his own professional football team.

It has been the privilege of the writers of this book to have known many Carlisle graduates and former students. Some of them—like the football coach and later Indian Bureau attorney Albert Exendine, a Delaware; Joe Pappio, a Chippewa, who became an electrician at Tinker Air Force Base, Oklahoma City, after many years of service with the Indian Bureau school system; and Jason Betzinez, a Chiricahua who was captured at the age of approximately twenty-one with Geronimo and who followed Pratt from Fort Marion to Carlisle, later to become post blacksmith at Fort Sill, Oklahoma—were successful in any man's terms and they never lost touch with their own people.

Betzinez married a white woman Mennonite missionary from Illinois. Until the day of his death at the age of one hundred and four, when he drove his automobile into a bridge abutment, he always spoke of Pratt as "my old general," and had a reverence for him that he had for no other person.

Then there were the failures. People returned to their families, whom they were supposed to influence to "follow the good way," unable to speak to anyone because English had totally replaced their native vocabularies. These poeple withdrew from life entirely, sitting silent and alone until death took them or finding refuge in the cheap whiskey sold in towns bordering the reservations. Or they turned their backs on Indian life altogether, found jobs in white communities working with whites, and refused to admit their racial origins, calling themselves "Spanish" or "Italian," or in extreme instances "Mexican" or "Negro."

But for every sorry failure there were modest and almost unnoticed successes. For many years it was possible to distinguish in Indian communities which women had been trained at Carlisle—by their housekeeping, their cooking, and above all their coffee. Such German dishes as hot potato salad, apple pie, and doughnuts still have their places on Indian as well as Pennsylvania German tables.

Carlisle graduates read the Bible and taught their children to do so. They sent their children to school automatically; that was the place where children should be. They attended mission churches of all denominations and encouraged their tribesmen to go with them. The battle was not so much to the strong as to the enduring.

And Carlisle had its social triumphs, too. A young New York State woman, Elaine Goodale, a teacher at the school, married one of the older Sioux students, Charles Eastman. He went on to become famous equally as a physician and as a writer, while his wife headed many Indian assistance movements. Her biography, *Pratt, The Red Man's Moses*, is still the main source for scholars of Pratt's life, although his autobiography, hidden or lost for many years after his death, has since been published. The Eastmans were received everywhere, including the White House, as honored and distinguished guests.

When Pratt was an old man in his eighties, and long retired from military service, "the General" visited the western states to see his old students. Betzinez told how he was unable to speak to his old general because he wept so with joy to see the man that words would not come. He was not alone. Pratt engendered devotion and loyalty among his students by his absolute fairness and impartiality. Rigid disciplinarian though he was, he was basically a kind and fair man, with a great human warmth.

The greatest achievement of Carlisle was that it set a pattern Indian Bureau schools could follow. Now there was precedent for certain types of training and organization, and it was a strong and impressive one.

On the other side of the ledger the ink is red. Families were broken up or broken into. Lives were disrupted or destroyed. Men and women who might have been leaders of their peoples in buffalo hunting days were humbled and defeated before they left Carlisle. Some contracted diseases which they liberally distributed among their peoples on their return. Children became strangers to their parents.

Much has been said and written about the psychological impact of such a school on children used to "freedom." Culture shock there certainly was, including the shock of reentry when the students left the artificial shelter of the school.

The interesting speculation is: What would have become of some of the Carlisle students if they had not gone away from home? Some were orphans without relatives who were able to care for them. Some girls were already sexually promiscuous and had to be watched while they were away. A few of these were sent home with the results of their "little accidents" wailing in their arms. Some boys, raised in a horse-stealing tradition, would have probably gone on stealing anything they could get their hands on. Similar boys steal untended automobiles today, and it is a strong public defender who can keep them out of jail. Who can weigh the value of one human life against another?

But a pattern of education had been established, and it continued all over the country. Government boarding schools were erected on and off reservations. The Carlisle plan of students' working part of each school day was followed, although it was not practical to install the "outing" plan. There were too few non-Indian families outside Pennsylvania who were willing to take Indians into their homes for the "outing" system to work elsewhere.

Many charges have been leveled against Indian Service schools, and unfortunately some of them are justified. There were Bureau superintendents, in some reservation areas particularly, who sent the police to bring in students and force them to attend school. Parents hid the children, and weeping pupils were hauled bodily from under beds, from holes in the ground over which mats or hides or blankets had been stacked, or, in the case of the Hopis, from corn storage jars, outdoor ovens, and even kivas.

This was bad enough, but school discipline was sometimes even worse. Carlisle discipline, based on that of the Army, aimed at making students self-sufficient and providing them with the rigid backbones they would need in later life. In many of the civilian schools disciplinaries took their roles too seriously and sometimes sadistically. For every Joe Pappio, a Bureau of Indian Affairs disciplinarian, who, when he found a boy napping in the hay barn, turned his head and went away quietly, only to return making a loud noise, and who spoke to and of the children as "my boys," there was a disciplinarian somewhere else who was out-and-out cruel.

Work hours were long and hard at some schools. Products from school farms, dairies, and bakeries were sold to merchants in nearby towns, and students lived on dried beans, rancid bacon, and cornbread instead of on the food they had helped produce and which they were intended to consume. Runaways were frequent, and food thefts were daily affairs. Hungry children must be fed.

Worst of all, though, was the low quality of education among the teachers. Carlisle instructors had been retired military men and their wives or earnest eager volunteers of good background and personal education. Under their tutelage, the students learned to speak good English, to write beautifully in a flowing Spencerian hand, and to read for the sheer pleasure of reading.

It was not until the 1930's that civil service requirements for teachers in Bureau schools included a college degree with at least a minor in educational method, as well as a major in the subject to be taught.

Until then, school principals were often men who had been successful in teaching farming to adults or businessmen who knew little or nothing of education but, having failed in other endeavors, were looking for an easy job. Not until the middle 1930's was an in-service training plan instituted for teachers, or were teachers encouraged to raise the level of their own educations and thereby their salaries.

Indians were given preference, in the form of 25 percent credit, on Civil Service examinations for Bureau positions. This meant that sometimes more capable or better-informed non-Indian teachers had to be passed over in order that a less-qualified Indian might receive an appointment. Later, Indian students who reached college expected an additional 25 percent in grade points "because they were Indians."

The Five Civilized Tribes maintained their own schools, selected their own teachers, and established their own standards until after 1900. Students went to these boarding schools willingly, even when the schools had been absorbed by the government. In general, the quality of education was both high and practical. Men and women who emerged from the Cherokee seminaries, the Choctaw boarding schools, the Creek, Chickasaw, and Seminole academies, were responsible and capable human beings.

They knew how to use both their heads and their hands, which could not be said of the average graduate of an Indian Bureau school at that time.

Mission boarding schools flourished in some parts of the country, with each sect establishing its own standards for teachers. Some of these schools, like the St. Mary's Girls' School established by the Episcopal Church in the Sioux country, or the Moravian and Presbyterian schools elsewhere, were excellent. St. Patrick's mission, among the Kiowa, run by Belgian monks, really made farmers out of boys whose fathers were horsemen, and who would otherwise, probably, have become Agency "coffee coolers." The same thing could be said of the work of other Catholic missions: Sacred Heart, among the Potawatomi, and some of the schools in the Osage country, especially. Other church schools were less desirable.

By far the biggest and most far-reaching influence for education among the adult Indians was the work of the "agency farmers" and "field matrons." These men and women took the places since held by agricultural demonstration agents. Field matrons were more than home demonstration agents, however. They taught canning, cooking, and sewing, but they also nursed the sick, transported those who needed more than home nursing to hospitals, sobered up drunken husbands, delivered babies, encouraged children to go to school and took them there and brought them home, and, in their spare moments, fostered arts and crafts. It is safe to say that wherever Indian art in its best form has survived in this country there was once a busy and interested field matron at work.

Kiowa art in particular, and Indian art in general, owes more to Susie Peters, once of Anadarko, Oklahoma, than to any other one person. A human dynamo in a tiny frame, Mrs. Peters bedeviled universities into accepting Indian students with less than high school educations into their art departments, and philanthropists into supporting the students while they were attending the universities. Single-handed, she built a whole school of Indian art, based on the pictographic drawings of the Kiowa year counts. From Oklahoma the style spread outward, until today, as has been said, it is considered "traditional" and "typical" by people of whom the Kiowa had never heard in Mrs. Peters' more active days.

With the added encouragement of Dr. Oscar Brouse Jacobson, of the University of Oklahoma, Dorothy Dunn, and Mable Morrow, both of the education division of the

Bureau of Indian Affairs, and of such philanthropists as Lew Wentz, Will Rogers, Judge and Mrs. William Denman, Mr. and Mrs. Charles De Young, and others, American Indian art became again something to be collected and treasured as it had not been since the days of the dauphins of France.

Hospitals, as well as schools, and health services generally had been promised in many treaties. From about 1900 on some hospitals were built, or medical care was given to Indians in Army hospitals. More often treatment was left in the hands of "contract doctors"—physicians in nearby towns who treated Indian patients in their offices or who visited Indian homes and were compensated by the government. Many of these men were of the highest quality, both personally and professionally, and it is unfortunate that the few who failed to meet the high standards of the many were the ones who were regarded as exemplifying the whole group.

Later, resident physicians employed by the Division of Indian Health, Bureau of Indian Affairs, were installed in Agency towns. These doctors were assisted by field nurses, who held outpatient clinics and prenatal and postnatal training courses for mothers and examined patients who could not be moved in their homes, reporting a need for additional care, where it existed, to the Agency doctor.

The Division of Indian Health pioneered in the use of sulfanilamide in the treatment of trachoma, an eye disease that had threatened whole tribes with blindness and could be miraculously cured by the new drug. The Division of Indian Health struggled with local medical societies, with Congressional appropriations to assist and support their work, and with the Indians themselves.

For it was uphill all the way in many areas. Navaho and Apache, as well as Kiowa and Cheyenne, stayed away from the new hospitals in droves. People had died in those buildings, and the uneasy spirits of the dead were believed to haunt the hospital halls. It was safer to stay at home and submit to the treatment of the "Indian doctor," whom the non-Indians called the medicine man.

Sometimes a piece of quick and observant thinking saved the day—and thousands of lives. At Ganado, Arizona, the Presbyterian Church established a mission hospital. Here the resident physician called in Navaho singers, or priest-doctors, to take part in the hospital's dedication. From time to time, after a death, the singers were recalled to cleanse the atmosphere spiritually.

The separate Indian Health Division was to be superseded in 1955 by the United States Public Health Service. In many ways, as tending to relieve the automatic segregation of reservation or allotted areas, this was a good thing. Often the same personnel were transferred from one government agency to another, and the same people went on working at the same jobs.

The administrative and titular change was bitterly resented by many Indians, however. Their treaties had promised them their own health service, and now it had been taken away—another violation of the already-abrogated treaties.

To discuss any government bureau objectively is a difficult thing. The Bureau of Indian Affairs is responsible not only for health and educational services but for soil conservation, maintenance of law and order in reservation areas, training in agriculture and home economics, construction of roads and buildings, and a multimillion-dollar nationwide banking business. It has no "wards," but it does collect, deposit, and pay out funds for individuals and tribes.

Inevitably, in such a chain of activities, conducted solely by human beings, there are weak links. Occasionally one snaps. There has been fraud and corruption, an outstanding example of which is the Tea Pot Dome oil scandal of the 1920's. The Bureau employees themselves broke open the even more shocking chain of insurance murders on the Osage reservation in north central Oklahoma, which occurred at about the same time.

Good, bad, and sometimes woefully indifferent, the employees of the Bureau have passed their Civil Service examinations and have qualified for the positions they hold. They are not, as is sometimes asserted, despots who "shut the Indians up on reservations."

Reservation areas were originally established to protect the Indians from non-Indian exploitation. From the beginning of the Bureau, before the ratification of the United States Constitution, the men and women who have worked for it have faced discomfort, isolation, meager living conditions, and small salaries on which to support families. The best and the worst qualities of human beings emerge under such circumstances.

22

Determination

THE NINETEENTH CENTURY, PARTICULARLY IN GERmany, England, and the United States, combined cold-blooded materialism with sentimental romanticism. Railroads *must* cross the continent, at whatever cost in lives, starvation, suffering, cultural shock, and emotional readjustment. And cross it they did.

At the same time, not only was the sense of guilt with which our own century is overfamiliar aroused, but there was a burning urge on the part of certain people to do something about the condition of the Indians.

Short of legislating the non-Indian population of the country out of existence and allowing matters to return to the status quo of pre-1100, there was little that could really be accomplished. Missionaries, contract doctors, and field matrons and nurses did the best they could, as we have seen. But ladies' church circles, cultural clubs, and other righteous bodies felt that a wrong had been perpetrated, and it was their duty to undo it.

So boxes of old clothes were collected and sent to reservations. Silks and satins were hardly appropriate wear, but they were worn. Hats were rejected entirely, except by men who farmed their fields under the shade of ostrich plumes, or Osage brides who decorated men's top hats with plumes or banderillas. Thin-soled, high-heeled slippers and shoes were far from appropriate for walking on rough ground, but they were worn when a pair could be found to fit—somewhere in the bottom of the box. Soap and staple groceries were seldom, if ever, included. It was assumed that they could be obtained anywhere.

Collections were taken up, and Indian children were "sponsored" or "adopted" by non-Indian families. Nothing particular was done to get these children into schools, on or off the reservations, but they did receive expensive toys at Christmas, together with clothes suitable for play on Boston Common or in Central Park.

College scholarships for Indian students had been established by many eastern colleges at the beginning of the century. A few had been used, but, in the main, Indian students were too poorly prepared for college work to take advantage of them. The absolute removal of all restrictions except those imposed by the particular school in question brought no improvement to students who were accustomed to being fighting men or married women by the time they reached fifteen, and now found themselves being treated as youths who must be sheltered from the rough exposures of an alien world.

There was hardly anywhere the more realistic approach of giving scholarships to grade and high school students. Scholarships meant to most people college scholarships, for superior young men and women, not books and shoes and warm clothing for first and second graders.

At the same time, attention had at last been directed to the nonmaterial essentials of Indian life. Lewis Henry Morgan, like Benjamin Franklin and Thomas Jefferson before him, explored the legal intricacies of the Iroquois system of government. Henry Rowe Schoolcraft, himself married to a half-Chippewa, learned his wife's language and the ways of her people; then went on, as a special representative of the Department of the Interior to learn the lifeways of other Indians.

The fruit of Schoolcraft's labor was six massive, unindexed tomes put out by Lippincott and Company in Philadelphia in 1860. These volumes set a model for future publications of the newly created Bureau of Ethnology. Later this unit became, under the Smithsonian Institution's auspices, the Bureau of American Ethnology. And in the twentieth century an ethnologist would receive his PH.D. degree for performing the monumental task of indexing Schoolcraft's work.

The index was a hundred years in the future, and in the meantime a boy was growing up in northern New York State. Frail from birth and a loner by nature, Frank Hamilton Cushing wandered the woods, picking up chipped stone artifacts, reading Morgan and Schoolcraft before he was in his teens, and endlessly wondering about the men who had walked the woods before him. He was educated at home, and largely self-educated after he passed the three R's.

One day young Cushing read a newspaper. That would not ordinarily be an event, but the boy was not given to newspaper reading, and it happened that this particular journal contained an article on an expedition about to set out, from the still-new Smithsonian Institution, to explore the southwest and to bring back "reports and artifacts" from the peoples native to the region. The expedition would be under the command of Lieutenant James Stevenson, and his wife, Matilda Coxe Stevenson, would accompany him as "ethnologist"—a new word to the Cushing vocabulary, but a word to which Cushing was to give more form and meaning than any other man.

Perhaps it was the presence of Stevenson's wife in the party that convinced Frank Cushing's mother that the expedition would be safe for her boy. Had she known the redoubtable Matilda, Mrs. Cushing might have thought differently. At any rate, Stevenson himself was well known as an explorer and frontiersman, and was said to be as familiar with the southwest as any Anglo-American of his time.

The boy traveled to Washington and began a series of pleas to the Stevensons. The presence of an extra civilian was not particularly welcome in a military expedition but the boy's earnestness at last won Lieutenant Stevenson over. Cushing was allowed to travel with the party—at his own and his family's expense, be it noted—as "assistant ethnologist." It was a turning point in the history of the American Indians, and the birth pang of a new science—cultural anthropology.

By train, by wagon train, and on horseback the party journeyed westward. When they could, they stayed at frontier Army posts, or with traders or missionaries. When there was no hospitable roof available, they camped out. Mrs. Stevenson preferred camping to missionaries, in any case. When there were no missionaries there were no embarrassing questions about the ten-gallon kegs of whiskey she had ordered lashed under the wagons.

At Zuni, where Coronado had met his first disappointment and near-defeat, the party separated. The Stevensons and their military escort continued westward, to the Hopi, or as Stevenson called them, "Moki," villages. Young Cushing was left behind at Zuni, to survive as best he could in a notoriously hostile community.

How he survived, and how he became accepted by the

people of Zuni, not only as one of them but as a high-priestly official, he later told in a series of articles published in the old *Century Illustrated Magazine* in 1882, and republished in book form as *My Adventures in Zuni,* by the Peripatetic Press of Sante Fe, New Mexico.

That Frank Cushing genuinely loved the people of Zuni, and that they genuinely loved him, there is no doubt. When the Stevenson party returned and he had to leave his new family, Cushing and the Indians alike wept. He would return again and again to that increasingly familiar place, and always afterward he signed his letters: "Ethnologist, Smithsonian Institution; Zuni Priest of the Bow."

The few remaining years of Frank Cushing's life—he died of tuberculosis at the age of forty-three—were spent in a state of cultural ambiguity that has since become familiar to many ethnologists. He was, as he said, a scientific anthropologist—as much as such a thing existed then—and a Zuni Priest of the Bow. He lectured and traveled widely, spreading the word that Indians were people and should be treated as people and not as soulless animals. He wrote voluminously, and in that more leisured period of time people read what he wrote, even in the unwieldy volumes the Bureau of American Ethnology continued to publish as its *Annual Reports* into the 1920's.

What Cushing wrote remains good reading today. He had style and flair, whatever he did: writing, excavation in Florida; presiding over the Bow Priests' kiva, or on an eastern lecture platform. Thomas Eakins painted his portrait, full length and life size, and it hangs today in the Thomas Gilcrease Museum of Indian Art, Tulsa, Oklahoma. It is the portrait of a handsome, mustachioed young man, his hair worn long and bound with a scarf across his forehead Zuni style, standing surrounded by his collection of Zuni art. The illness that was to cut short his life shows in his face, and so does the wistfulness of a man lost between two cultures, each equally valid to him.

If Cushing never resolved his own inner conflict, there were others who never experienced it. Lieutenant Stevenson collected artifacts and information impartially for many years, as did his wife. From the 1870's on, these two did much to shape the course of American anthropological studies of the American Indian; they wrote, published, and dominated the southwestern scientific scene until Matilda's death, long after her husband's, in 1914.

Other anthropologists took to the field. Alice Fletcher studied the Indians of the middle Mississippi Valley—

Omaha, Oto, Osage, and Ponce particularly—with an enthusiasm and identification that almost equaled Cushing's. Throughout the 1880's, with the assistance of the Omaha Laflesche family, her principal informants, Miss Fletcher was not content with merely recording tribal pasts; she set about to improve the sordid conditions in which other informants lived. There was nothing of the starry-eyed idealist about Alice Fletcher. She thought conditions of Indian life were, in the main, deplorable, and she said so.

That, in turn, leads us back to the people who guiltily, earnestly, honestly *tried* to help the Indians. Had these people listened to what Cushing and Miss Fletcher did *not* say, they would have accomplished more.

Audiences heard a strange mélange of spiritual richness in mythology, ceremony, prayer, and legend combined with material deprivation of a kind that made their blood run cold. People accustomed to the amenities and comforts of life could not believe that other people would not welcome the material existence by which they were themselves surrounded.

In actual fact, as an old Hopi priest said to the writers of this book, "The Indians were better off before people like you began worrying so much about them. Before, we had food and clothing and shelter. They were ours; we were used to them and we liked them. Then the missionaries and the schoolteachers came and told us we were deprived. We began to wonder about that. Pretty soon we saw that there were things like pianos and mirrors to want. We learned to be discontented, and our children and grandchildren don't know what contentment is. We lived with the world of animals and plants, and we were happy."

This wistful plea for the return of the days that never were is familiar to all of us. Childhood often becomes in memory a time of enchantment—even to people who hated every frustrating minute of it.

Indians knew envy, hatred, malice and all uncharitableness long before the New World was invaded. Myths and legends clearly demonstrate that fact. The tussel over the Mississippi Valley between the Athabascans and the Iroquoians, that would inevitably have come had Europeans stayed on their own side of the Atlantic Ocean, is clearly foreshadowed in the earliest records of both peoples.

Indians were and remained human. Their resources were those of the world around them. They made their ways of life from those natural resources, like everybody else—and the dreams of old men are longer than the thoughts of youth. Naturally the old Hopi remembered the good and forgot the bad. But the bad had been there, even in the best of times.

The southwestern states are excellent places in which to recover from asthma, arthritis, bronchial ailments, and tuberculosis, and by 1900 "cures" in such places as Santa Fe and Phoenix had become fashionable. Living was not particularly expensive for those who could live at home, and sanatariums generally charged less for treatment than similar institutions in the east.

People who were under treatment or in process of recovery from severe illnesses soon discovered the Indians. Some were motivated by genuine delight in and affection for the high, dry country with its crisp, clean winters and not-too-hot summers. They liked the place and wanted to stay there, and they wanted to know its people. They set out to learn "the things the anthropologists never get to know," and when the patients returned to their homes they took with them tales of their esoteric encounters. The natural quiet—the graciousness—of the village peoples added an illusion of intimacy. Illusion it was.

Artists, too, were drawn to the clean forms of the land, the beauty of its inhabitants. There was a "Taos school" of art, a "Santa Fe school," an "Albuquerque school," and today there is the "Scottsdale school," located geographically between Phoenix and Tucson.

Artists found readier acceptance among the southwestern Indians than did other non-Indians, perhaps because they shared the gifts of the hands. Some writers, especially those who learned against all Anglo impulses to sit still and keep quiet, could find acceptance. But it was acceptance of a special sort; there was always a wall of reserve between Indians and non-Indians of whatever occupation.

The southwest gained fame as the word spread eastward that here was the earthly paradise, the place where men and nature merged—in comfortable houses, not too far from good restaurants and well-staffed bars. The impact of this form of white invasion wrought as deep an impression on the Indian life of the southwest as had the plowing of the Plains on the Indians of that area. Tourism was big business, and nobody has forgotten that fact for a moment.

Few visitors stopped to consider that the women who crouched on railroad station platforms or sheltered under their shawls beside highways, offering pottery for sale, were, in a sense, committing artistic prostitution. The wares made for home use, for utility, whether decorated or not, had about them a sturdiness and honesty that the paint-smeared "rain gods" and their counterparts could never have.

Those economic opportunists, the Navaho, soon learned that blankets woven with cotton string warps and commercial yarn wefts could be produced more quickly, looked smoother, and sold just as well as those honestly made with hand-spun yarns throughout their fabric. Silver-and-turquoise jewelry did not have to be set with turquoise. Blue glass would do just as well. The silver itself need not have the massive sculptural quality the Indians demanded for their own wearing. Sheet silver could be cut up more easily than coins or mint slugs could be pounded flat. In fact, sheet silver could be rolled even thinner than the weight at which it was sold.

A Navaho wore his bank account on his person. If times were lean, he pawned a belt or a necklace at a trading post, took the proceeds for immediate use, and tried to redeem the piece within the year if he could. If he could not, the trader was free to put the pawned piece up for sale, although many established traders have kept pieces in pawn for generations, lending the jewelry back to its owner or his heirs when a special occasion demanded special finery. The loaned pieces of pawn were honorably returned to their custodians.

"It's safer to have silver in the vault at the trading post than lying around the hogan," a member of the Navaho tribal council once explained, "and you can get tired carrying all that hardware around with you."

Nonetheless, it became fashionable for newly inducted southwesterners to denigrate the traders as exploiters of the poor ignorant Indians, "who charged twice as much for a sack of flour as they paid for it."

That 100 percent markups were not uncommon among other merchants in other parts of the United States, that many traders carried families year after year on credit, and that they were the only non-Indians except professional linguists who made a conscious effort to learn Indian languages, and so do business to the greater comfort of the Indians—these aspects were not taken into consideration by the attackers. The traders were condemned by the uninformed as a pack of thieves, taking advantage of the poverty and ignorance of the majority of their customers.

The professional Indian specialists split among themselves. Archaeologists excavated large portions of the landscape and found a wide variety of pottery styles. Every sherd became a site, and every archaeologist vigorously defended his own nomenclature against all comers. An archaeologist looked down his nose at ethnologists, who were concerned with "all that contemporary junk." The ethnologists, toilsomely producing technical descriptions of kinship and social systems, varied with occasional forays into ethnopornography, despised the archaeologists, "who don't know what *real* Indian life is like."

D. H. Lawrence, professional writer, amateur painter, and apostle of gloom, mourned from his citadel above Taos in the 1920's that the Indians were "unapproachable." They had a "deep blackness" that no non-Indian could penetrate. The Indians of Taos Pueblo retorted that Lawrence was a "real sick man," the worst thing any Indian could say of anyone.

The battle of ideologies raged back and forth within the southwestern teapot, and unfortunately its waves spread outward and reached the coast of either ocean.

It would be interesting to compile a list of associations formed to "help the Indian" since the middle nineteenth century. They come and they go. Some wield considerable legislative influence and have been instrumental as lobbying groups. They have done much good and not a little bad. But whatever they have done, these associations, societies, or whatever they may have called themselves have done it with vigor, enthusiasm, and plenty of publicity.

It has become a mark of distinction among these amateurs to "live on a reservation," to "eat with the Indians," and to attend ceremonies where "there isn't another white man in miles."

Professional anthropologists seldom mention such things, and certainly do not brag about them. Not only are serious investigators received in Indian homes; they bring Indian guests into their own houses. But this is all in the day's work, and not to be mentioned except casually, in conversation with a fellow anthropologist.

It is hard for professional ethnologists, who enter Indian lives to observe, learn, and report, to be objective. The non-participant observer is the unobtainable ideal. The presence of any outsider in any community automatically alerts that community's structure and the interrelationships of the persons who comprise it. The effect on Indian lives of a person who visits for three days and goes away an expert is deplorable. And when the self-proclaimed expert, who undoubtedly has formed acquaintanceships during his brief stay, loudly announces that the Indians "among whom he has lived" are exploited, downgraded, and humiliated by non-Indians, other uninformed persons believe him. In time, even the Indians have been convinced that they are "second-class citizens."

Indians divide themselves into four classes today: professional Indians, powwow Indians, political Indians, and just people.

True it is that when United States citizenship—bestowed first in 1871 with the final abrogation of treaties—was reconfirmed for all American Indians in recognition for their services in the armed forces during the 1916–1918 war, there were still Indians who were denied the right to vote. The United States Constitution, trying to bring order out of Federalist chaos, had specifically stated that each state should set its own requirements for voters. Jim Crow laws applied to Indians as well as to Negroes in many states.

It was not until 1948, when a Tewa-speaking Pueblo Indian proved in court that by buying a package of cigarettes he had automatically become a taxpayer, that Indians received the right to vote in New Mexico. A similar case, concerning state sales taxes, was fought through the courts two years later in Arizona, to prove that that state's Indians were citizens enfranchised in the state as well as in the nation.

Whether or not a voter is informed of his rights and privileges under the laws and whether he cares to exercise his franchise are different matters. It is true that many Indian today *do not vote*. It is not true that they *cannot* vote.

Anthropologists, clambering from their investigative remoteness to the lecture platform, had inadvertently drawn attention to living and educational conditions that many people rightly considered inadequate and insufficient for any citizens of the richest country in the world. Whether or not the anthropologists intended such a result is debatable. They were first trying to present the facts they had laboriously gathered.

The result is there, confronting us. Indian life in the United States has been deeply and finally affected by those who set out, in good earnest, to study and report on it, as well as by those inspired with a crusading zeal to right the wrongs of all the world.

Consequently, no idea is more widespread than the notion that when the treaties between European governments or the United States and various Indian groups were broken, the Indians' spirits broke simultaneously. No idea could be a greater misconception. Indians themselves broke treaties from time to time, and never did they offer more than token submission to stronger forces.

From the day in 1675 when Metacomet—King Philip—led his Narragansett against the English, to 1969, when the National Congress of American Indians, an intertribal group, began readying its next assault on the Congress of the United States, and the American Indians—United organized in Chicago to teach urban Indians to be "bi-cultural," there was always resistance of one sort or another. If there had not been resistance, there would be no recognizable Indian groups in this country today.

Powhatan was set to dong Captain John Smith on the head and so end the southeastern Indians' English invasion, when Powhatan's daughter, Pocahontas, like the spoiled child she was, demanded the Englishman as a plaything. Had Indian parenthood generally not been so permissive in its attitudes, the history of the southern settlements might have taken a far different course. By saving one Englishman, Pocahontas saved them all. She did not succeed in preventing future bloody strife between invaded and invaders.

Even the Pueblo, meek and peaceful incarnations of the average man that they claimed to be, could stand the Spaniards just so long and no longer. The Pueblo rebellion of 1692 was not put down until ten years later, and New Mexico was far from safe in Spanish hands for at least another century.

Tsali of the Cherokees, his wife, Amanda, and their sons chose death at the hands of the Georgia militia rather than surrender their lands. They were not alone; the other civilized tribes had their resistance heroes, too. Osceola the Seminole led his people in and out of the southern swamps, harassing as much as harassed, until his capture and subsequent death of loneliness. No, the Indians did not sit down and meekly accept defeat. Kentucky was not named dark and bloody ground for nothing.

Tecumseh, the Shawnee war leader, and his twin brother, Tenskwautawa, the Prophet, tried before the War of 1812 to organize the northern tribes against the forces of the United States. Their attempt proved abortive, but it did have the effect of adding Indian volunteers to the British forces and thus prolonging a war that the English themselves regarded as a side issue to a major conflict with France.

In 1832 Black Hawk, the Sauk and Fox war leader, urged rebellion and resistance among his people and the affiliated Algonquian tribes, Potawatomi, Shawnee, and Kickapoo, in the northern Mississippi Valley. Again the effort was defeated, and the principal fact that most Americans remember today about the Black Hawk War is that Abraham Lincoln served in it as a private of the Illinois militia. Black Hawk's magnificent speech of defiance to Andrew Jackson at the conclusion of hostilities, "I am a man and you are nothing more," has been forgotten, as has the fact that Jackson presented Black Hawk with a silver peace medal as a token of esteem.

In the end, inevitably, superior technology had its way. Reservations were set aside for Indian tribes. Later, lands were to be allotted in severalty to some groups, in which case each member of the allotted tribe or band would receive 160 acres of his own—enough land to feed twelve steers in the potential dust bowl, whatever it may have produced in lush Pennsylvania or Illinois.

Resistance continued with the Modoc war of 1870, the Plains wars of that whole decade, the sullen refusal of the affiliated Caddo, Wichita, Wea, and Tawakoni to do anything at all, after their removal from Texas to present western Oklahoma, but sit down on their lands and pout. When the occasion offered, the Caddoan groups would seize the opportunity to burn and loot government buildings.

In fact, resistance continued into the twentieth century, and Chitto Harjo—Crazy Snake—led a handful of Creek warriors in the last armed Indian rebellion against the United States, near Seminole and Wewoka, Indian territory. The Creek nation, Chitto said, should never become a part of any state, particularly not one with the lying Choctaw name of Oklahoma (Land of the Red Men).

A more frequent form of resistance than fighting was dancing. In 1870 a Paiute named Wovoka, or Jack Wilson, who had been adopted by a family of white settlers and educated in non-Indian culture, announced a vision. He had seen the Christ, he said, and had been personally assured that he was himself an incarnation of the messiah.

Undoubtedly Wovoka had seen, physically, members of the non-Indian Shaker cult of Washington and Oregon, who danced themselves into trancelike oblivion to the music of bells clutched in their shaking hands. Such dancing, Wovoka proclaimed, could bring back the dead, the buffalo, and the whole old way of life—together with the elimination of the whites who were the cause of all the Indians' miseries.

The messianic cult grew and spread throughout the Great Basin and Plateau areas, from Nevada, Washington, and Oregon through Nebraska and the Dakotas.

Then the Ghost Dance seemed to die away and be forgotten. But the idea behind it persisted, and messianic cults continued to grow and spread throughout the Plains.

The Brulé, Miniconjou, Hunkpapa and Oglala Sioux, like the Arapaho and Cheyenne, embraced the cult. By 1892 almost twenty years after Wovoka first announced his vision, these always warlike peoples were seething with humiliations and indignations. They were confined to reservation areas where, even if there had been buffalo left to hunt, there was no room for hunting.

Children were taken as hostages and sent away to school, to return after ten-year spans as "imitation white men." Most of these tribes existed on treaty-promised handouts of poor food and worse clothing. The Sun Dance, the center of their religious life and year cycle, had been forbidden because of its self-torture elements. In short, there was little left of the old life of the Plains and no promise of success or happiness for these Indians in the new culture.

As they had done in 1849 when the first California-bound migrants crossed their lands, the Sioux, the Cheyenne, and the Arapaho of the northern Plains danced. This time it was not to release tensions, but rather to build them up.

Wearing white cotton garments, painted with protective signs of the sun, moon, and stars to make them bulletproof, the Indians danced the moon down and the sun up. They fell into trances and communed with their beloved dead. Round and round the Ghost Dancers circled, men and women together, building toward a mighty climax when all the tribes should rise, united, and in armed rebellion to do away with their conquerors and bring the old days back.

In the southern Plains, Ahpeahtone (Wooden Lance), a Kiowa peace chief, had recently lost a daughter. He, too, hoped to bring her back to life. A true Kiowa pragmatist, he went first to investigate the Ghost Dance at its source. The dance had already reached the southern Cheyenne and Arapaho, who were busily dancing all night and getting their weapons ready all day, against the time when the signal for armed revolt should come.

The story of Ahpeahtone's travels northward is itself an epic. He traveled by train from one reservation area to another. Everywhere he went, people fed him, housed him for a few days, and sent him forward to the Paiute country and Wovoka.

Here Ahpeahtone discovered not the messiah the Baptist missionaries had described to the Kiowa, but a man like other men, who took women as he wanted them and lived anything but a saintly life. Ahpeahtone's hopes of resurrection were dashed, and he returned to his people convinced that only through the good life and the attainment of the Baptists' heaven could he find his daughter again. He persuaded the other Kiowa to accept the Ghost Dance as a social dance, not a religious one.

Since the Kiowa have never been known to unite on anything, some of them danced themselves into the trance state in the northern way, but they did not arm themselves —they only hoped to prepare the way for Armageddon. Years later, when he was an old man, the United States awarded Ahpeahtone a pension for his courage in combating what could have been a widespread Plains war.

Another form of resistance was to turn one's back on unbearable conditions and return physically to the homeland. The struggle of Dull Knife's band of northern Cheyenne from Oklahoma to Montana, in 1879, is another such epic. Nothing stopped them: barbed wire, railroads, imprisonment, starvation, and the deaths of their children were endured stoically until at last they reached the Yellowstone and stayed there, in the shadow of the Little Big Horn, not far from the scene of their greatest triumph—the Custer battlefield.

As time went on, and education had its pervasive way, Indians began to see that there was a point in joining them if you couldn't lick them. Men and women of education and good family held the Five Civilized Tribes together and became the intermediaries for the poverty-stricken illiterates who could not directly reach the ears of "Woosinton." Dominant their families had always been and dominant their descendants remained. Like their ancestors, these tribal leaders became the "talking chiefs" who spoke to outsiders.

Whether the influence of such tribal leaders was for bad or for good is not possible to say. They speak publicly now, as always, of "our poor Indian people," and they make decisions and plans for the underlings, without giving the others a voice in tribal affairs beyond token recognition of their existence.

A common expression among those who are united in the intertribal council of the Five Civilized Tribes, a body composed of less than a hundred members, became: "They have holes in their roofs, back there in the hills, that you could throw a dog through," and this was eventually transmuted to a shout of: "Here comes that damned dog again!" when a speaker arose to lament the woes of his followers.

By 1904 tribal rolls probably included as many non-Indians as Indians among the Five Civilized Tribes. Men and women of Caucasian birth who had married Indians were enrolled as full bloods. So were Negro slaves owned by the Indians, who were freed at the end of the Civil War, and their descendants.

Tribal leaders, both Indians and "intermarrieds," petitioned Congress for the formation of "an all-Indian state," the state of Sequoyah. This would have comprised the eastern half of the present state of Oklahoma. A constitution was written and tribal laws were codified. Then political pressure was exerted on Congress to include the western half of the state with the eastern half. It had already received the Choctaw name of Oklahoma. The constitution was slightly modified, the codified laws of the United States were adopted, and on November 16, 1907, the state of Oklahoma was admitted to the Union, although its population could not be said to be united within itself.

The western tribes were slower in their acculturation and sometimes less adroit at political manipulation than their eastern neighbors, but they began to see what legislative power could do. The Kiowa and Comanche in particular elected members to the state and national legislative bodies.

Politicians began to go out to beg for the Indian vote, and a sense of power pervaded the air at election times. The idea of the power of the Indian vote spread northward, as one state after another followed the example of the national Congress and enfranchised its Indian citizens. Charles Curtis, a Kaw, became Vice President of the United States. Houston B. Teehee, a Cherokee, was for many years Treasurer of the United States. His elegant Spencerian signature appeared on millions of dollars' worth of treasury notes. There was much pointing with pride and recital of "our Indian heritage."

Still resistance went on, in one form or another. An ancient Aztec religion wound its way northward from central Mexico to the southern Plains, gaining momentum and new culture traits as it went. In particular, the peyote religion acquired Christian elements in its travels.

From the Yaqui to the Apache; from the Apache and Yaqui to the Comanche; from Apache and Comanche to the Kiowa, and then by a mighty jump—a Winnebago visitor who traveled by train—to the Great Lakes it went. Back again down the Mississippi River and westward to the upper Missouri the peyote religion spread. Wherever it went, it met with resistance of its own. Wherever it is, there are Indians as well as non-Indians who resent and fear the Native American Church today.

"A peyote man has poor (thin) horses," an Arapaho said. "A real man takes care of his stock and feeds them before he eats himself. A peyote man knocks himself out at an all-night meeting, and can't feed anybody before noon."

Periodically, investigations have been made into the use of peyote and its effects since the late nineteenth century, and are still continuing; Congressional investigations are not an invention of the twentieth century; they have been with us always. From its inception the Bureau of Indian Affairs, under its different aliases and administrations, has been constantly investigated.

Investigation began, indeed, before the Revolution, when English colonial governors, notably Sir William Johnson, began sending missionaries and others to look into the lives and living conditions of the League of the Iroquois. To quote from all the reports written "on the conditions of the Indians" is impossible in the space available.

During the century and a half that Indian affairs bounced back and forth between civilian and military administrations, each group periodically investigated the other.

A few of the investigative attempts can be mentioned: that of Henry Rowe Schoolcraft in the early 1800's; Jedediah Smith's a few years later; the Grant investigation under General O. O. Howard, after the Civil War; the special agents, known in the Bureau as Big Cats, between 1880 and 1910; the Dawes Commission's inquiries into the enrollments of the Five Civilized Tribes, between 1900 and 1905; the report of the Brookings Institute Commission headed by Lewis Merriam, 1926–1927, which brought about a profound and scholarly report and some sweeping changes.

In 1933 Congress passed the Thomas-Rogers Bill applying to Oklahoma, and the Wheeler-Howard Indian Rights Act, applying to Indian tribes in other states and territories. These were directly the result of the efforts of John Collier, who had been appointed commissioner of Indian Affairs by President Franklin D. Roosevelt. Under these bills it was possible for Indian tribes to organize, draw up constitutions, and receive charters as incorporated bodies under state and federal laws. The Indian Arts and Crafts Board, directly under the Secretary of the Interior, was authorized by Congress. Tribal corporations dealt in everything from livestock to glass beads.

In 1934 the Indian Rights Association, under its president, Oliver La Farge, presented a symposium on the status of Indian affairs at that time. Later the symposium was published under the title *The Changing Indian*, by the University of Oklahoma Press.

Other commissioners of Indian Affairs had visited "Indian country," but Collier was indefatigable. His small wiry body, encompassing an unholy amount of energy, was likely to be found bouncing from reservation to allotted lands to Indian schools, erratically and unpredictably.

His successor, Glenn Emmons, of Gallup, New Mexico, and Emmons' successor, Dillon Myer, traveled widely but with less suddenness. Collier's stated aim had been "to work the government out of the Indian business," by making the Indians self-sustaining. His goal was to adapt tribal traditions and social orders to the twentieth century by introducing corporations whose charters were based on old organizations. There were some puzzles, of course, like that of the old man who inquired, "When you talk about stocks in a corporation, which do you mean: horses or cattle?"—but these could be dealt with.

Emmons and Myer took the same view but with a somewhat different approach. Indians were citizens of twentieth-century United States, and they should act that way, like everybody else. Somewhere and sometime the word "termination" was applied to government-reservation relations. It was caught up, with dread, by the Indians, who feared that they themselves, not land boundaries, might be "terminated."

"Mr. Commissioner, don't turn us a-loose," they pleaded in one meeting after another, but the processes of termination and relocation of families away from reservation and allotted areas continued.

Actually, of course, many Indians had already become self-relocated. The war of 1941–1945 had pulled both men and women into the military services. Families had "moved to town," where full employment opportunities were offered, away from the stunning idleness of the reservations. The process of adjustment from rural to urban living, while never easy, had been accomplished by the descendants of old tribal leaders, the persons who would have set the behavior pattern for others no matter how their society was organized.

At the same time, a strange ambiguity in government-tribal relations prevailed. Tribal members wanted self-determination at the same time that they fought against "termination."

The Indian Claims Commission had been established soon after World War II to settle once and for all the claims against the federal government for ceded or expropriated lands. Once a claim was heard and adjudicated, and payment in full was accepted by a tribe, that tribe as a corporate body ceased to exist. Its members were "terminated," and became citizens like other citizens, without the protection of a special bureau—the only bureau in recorded history, incidentally, ever established to protect the conquered from their conquerors. Claims against the federal government were based on traditions, and on boundaries established by treaties that had been abrogated almost a century before.

The Indian Claims Commission, since 1946, has paid out hundreds of millions of dollars in claims awards, and Congress has in each case appropriated the money for payment. Each time the members of the receiving tribe were begged by anyone who could attract an Indian ear to invest the money, to put it in savings bonds or accounts, or in group insurance, and each time the answer has been, "Thank you, but no thank you." One, three, five, two hundred million dollars had been appropriated to compensate a given tribe. Each tribesman was convinced that every penny of the entire sum belonged to him personally, and he was going to get his per capita share of the total, if he could not have the total, no matter what happened.

The game had swung full circle. Now the counters had changed hands. It was the non-Indians who fought to protect the intangibles: the art, the crafts, the music, the poetry. The Indians fought to hold the lands—or to sell them for the top price the market would bring. They wanted good solid dollars that they could spend for themselves.

Then, ironically, in 1950, the pendulum began to swing backward. Parents had struggled to live in cities and to provide non-Indian educations for their children. As the young men came back from war they wished to turn time back, to hold it again in the never-never land of tradition, song, and dance. Their parents seemed to have settled stodgily into middle-aged, middle-class comfort, solaced and supported in some cases by beer and cheap wine. Now youth was in the saddle, and it would create the better world.

The movement back took many forms. There were religious revivals, based, in many cases, on early anthropological descriptions in the annual reports of the Bureau of American Ethnology. State departments of education were besieged with requests to introduce Indian languages as "foreign languages" to meet school requirements. Textbooks for elementary schools in predominantly Indian communities were written phonetically, in Indian languages.

The powwow circuit was established. From Memorial Day to Labor Day it is possible to spend every weekend dancing and socializing, moving from one end of the country to the other, always welcome in the camps of other tribes. A good dancer or singer is welcome anywhere.

Out of this intertribal visiting coalitions began to form. The National Congress of American Indians had been organized in 1944, two years before the establishment of the Indian Claims Commission. Its purpose as first stated was to influence national legislation favorably to Indians. Following this example, the National Conference for American Indian Youth was called in the summer of 1961, in Boulder, Colorado.

In the cities, Indian Centers sponsored by the government, churches, and groups began to spring up, to meet the social and material needs of Indians who had settled in urban areas. These became the natural centers to which Indian youth gravitated; where plans could be made and carried out, and from which the word could spread that Indians were uniting against discrimination and segregation.

Was this true? Was there discrimination and segregation of Indians *because* they were Indians? Or did they feel an emotional ostracism because they did not cope as quickly with the complexities of urban existence as people who had been accustomed to it all their lives? Was this a fact, or an easy explanation for personal and group inadequacy? The answer probably is both.

On college campuses across the country "Black Power" began to be translated into "Red Power." One Seneca boy decided that since technological unemployment was steadily increasing in many skilled fields, there was really no reason for human beings to work at all. He invented a "thinking machine," a wonderful kinetic expression of revolving disks, flashing lights, and shifting planes, to carry from meeting to meeting with him.

"Look at it," the inventor would urge. "Watch the wheels go round. Pretty soon you won't feel anything at all. You won't have to think." And it was needless to argue with him that much thought had gone into the creation of the thinking machine and that there were, besides, people who *wanted* to think, not to be hypnotized.

Peyote, which had slipped into its place as a minority religion, was brought out into the light of the day. "Taking a trip" could be accomplished more easily with a sugar cube soaked in the peyote derivative, mescaline, than by eating a whole puckery button, but it was Native, American, and Churchly to consume it, all the same.

Alcoholism was another European-derived ailment from which American Indians had no immunity. For many years laws had been enacted to protect them from its damaging effects, and many tribal governments had also instituted rigid rules against the sale, purchase, or consumption of alcohol.

The returned servicemen protested against this restriction. "If you're old enough to fight, you're old enough to drink," they insisted. The repeal of national prohibition had paved the way. Soon any Indian who could afford it could purchase alcohol.

Drinking became another form of protest. The Native American Church had traditionally taken a firm stand against it, but now the younger people began to combine drinking and peyote—often with disastrous results. When one leader of "Indian youth" died of cirrhosis of the liver, the Department of the Interior auditorium was crowded to capacity with mourners who attended his memorial service.

"This man died a hero's death," one speaker proclaimed. "No longer can we ride out on our war horses to fight our enemies. Our battles today are of another kind. We can only die to win them."

Defeat? Victory? Or a step in a new direction?

In summary, how can we assess the positive contributions of American Indians to world culture? Most positively, in the field of horticulture. Corn, beans, squash—the three sisters that were the staples of American Indian diet. In medicine: cacao and its derivative pain-relievers; peyote and mescaline in the treatment of certain heart and emotional conditions. These last two might be open to question, as is tobacco, but the fact remains that their properties were known to Indians before the European landings. Tomatoes, potatoes both white and sweet, chili peppers—the list of plant foods derived from the New World is long and widespread.

It has been said that the Constitution of the United States was originally derived from the organization and functioning plan of the League of the Iroquois, and so it may have been. In that case it was certainly a positive contribution to the life of the United States.

Writers come to mind: the Osage John Joseph Mathews; the Cherokee playwright Lynn Riggs; the wit and humorist and wry observer Will Rogers, who not only thought about but felt the needs of the hill Cherokee, and who tried to relieve the worst of them by paying field nurses and doctors and social workers out of his own pocket; and above all, those magnificent translators of documents written in the Cherokee syllabary, Jack and Anna Kilpatrick; Muriel Wright, editor of the scholarly *Chronicles of Oklahoma;* the Kiowa Scott Momaday, recent Pulitzer Prize winner in fiction; Alex Posey, the Creek poet, and a host of others.

The field of applied, plastic, and graphic arts is filled to overflowing with the names of Indian painters and sculptors, many of them only now reaching the prime of their skill, and all constantly influencing and being influenced by one another. Their names are legion and the list of them will never be complete.

Will Rogers again heads the list of "show people," but the Oklahoma Indian ballerinas must be mentioned: Yvonne Chouteau, Maria and Marjorie Tallchief, Rosella and Marie Hightower, and Marcelle Larkin all have international reputations. Four of them: Chouteau, Marjorie Tallchief, Rosella Hightower, and Larkin have appeared with the Oklahoma City and Tulsa symphonies and the civic ballet groups of both cities in the ballet *Four Moons.* This was especially composed for them by Quapaw musician Louis Ballard.

Ballard also composed a ballet, *Koshari,* based on Pueblo mythology, which has been presented by the touring company of the Harkness Ballet.

Kilpatrick was also a composer, including a symphony to celebrate the Oklahoma semicentennial. He headed the department of musicology at Southern Methodist University in Dallas. He also deserves mention for his serious studies of the interactions of the music of Indian groups with one another.

Whether one considers rock 'n' roll music an art or an endurance contest is a matter of individual taste. Some contemporary composers claim to have been influenced by "the rolling beat of the tom-toms." Kilpatrick, as a serious musician, knew that tom-toms do not roll and are unknown in Indian music in any case. Nor are Indian drums rolled; Indian music generally is played in a steady one-two beat, never rising above a two-four, and always carefully controlled. Drums and rattles are differently pitched, and some drums may be reversed to change the pitch, in which case an entire chorus of singers will surge upward five tones in unison, producing an effect of syncopation, but without the variation of beat familiar in African and Afro-American music. Kilpatrick was working on a symphony, using only Indian musical patterns, at the time of his death in 1967.

Euro-American concepts of Indian life have undoubtedly influenced "the freedom thing" that has disrupted communities and campuses in the 1960's. Once again the Plains Indian stands before the world as the symbol of the untrammeled man. Serious students of Indian life in Europe form powwow clubs, design and make painfully authentic costumes, and devote years to the study of Indian music and dance, but this is a different matter from the "freedom revolt" and the invocation of Red Power.

Indian fashions have influenced the clothing of American women since the first adaptations of designs were presented by Neiman-Marcus of Dallas in 1938 and by the Indian Arts and Crafts Board at the Museum of Modern Art, New York City, in 1941.

A return of these styles is apparent in the 1960's: "soul beads" made by stringing juniper berries, which are providing a good living for some Navaho groups in southern Utah—and a good laugh for the same Navaho at the same time; it is not the first occasion that those cultural vacuum cleaners have taken advantage of change in style. Beaded as well as fabric headbands are being worn, and with them furred, feathered, and beaded leather clothing, sometimes dripping fringe, have appeared. The skins are prepared by European tanning methods, it is unnecessary to say.

Actual Indian clothing, worn in a New York hotel lobby in 1968, provoked no more comment than a muttered, "Which of the United Nations did *they* come from?" Until and unless designers return, as Lilly Daché and F. A. Picard did in the 1930's, to original, documented Indian clothing, it seems unlikely that the influence of Indian on non-Indian fashions will be more than temporary and superficial.

For real influence of American Indian life on that of the contemporary United States, we must go back to the beginnings; to the unknown artists who carved the ghostly totem poles and masks of the northwest. We must look again at the monumental pipes and the exquisitely incised pottery of the southeast; the delicate double curves of the ribbon appliqué and beadwork of the Great Lakes and the Mississippi Valley, and the infinite variety of fine design styles in the pottery, textiles, and jewelry of the southwest. We must hear again Black Hawk's proud declaration, "I am a man and you are nothing more," and Chief Joseph of the Nez Perce summoning tribal leaders to conference: "Hear me, my chiefs, my heart is heavy with oppression and I must speak to you of this thing."

It is in their oratory and their oral literature that the Indians have left their lasting monument, and it shall endure. As long as a Hopi priest of eighty-five can compose music that sends a famous European-born composer of the same age out of the plaza, sobbing, "Oh, God, if only I could ever have done that!" Indian arts and contributions to the arts must be considered living, and therefore unfinished, contributions to the world.

As this has been written a new administration has been installed in office, and a new Secretary of the Interior has assumed the thankless job of mediation among Indian groups. A journalistic survey, within two months of the inauguration, suggests putting the administration of Indian affairs directly under the President of the United States. One can only ask of the future: Whither?

Acknowledgments

No one or two persons could or should have written this book. It has been the work of many hearts and hands and minds besides our own. More than forty-five years of collective research, in the form of living experiences, have gone into it.

Whilc many volumes have been consulted, and the actual bibliography runs to an appalling length, still, in the last analysis, it has been the people we have known, the living processes of field experience, that have shaped our thinking and our expression of it.

We first thank, then, our Indian friends, but we do not list their names. The oldest of them are dead now, and their names therefore should not be spoken or written. We would not cause hurt or offense by unintentional omission. To all of you, then, we say as Cheyenne, Hah-hoh!

Our thanks go to our colleagues and administrators at Central State College, Edmond, Oklahoma, who aided in our research and who adjusted class assignments to make this work possible.

To the late John Collier, René d'Harnoncourt, Willard Beatty, Frederic Douglas, and Chester Faris, who made the United States Bureau of Indian Affairs (under the title of the United States Indian Service) and the Indian Arts and Crafts Board of the Department of the Interior instruments for human development and enrichment, wherever they have gone now they have left us, we give our thanks and promise to try to continue the work they began.

To the Hagerly Museum of Wilmington, Delaware, to

Philbrook Art Center and the Gilcrease Museum of Indian Art, Tulsa, Oklahoma, to the historical societies, museums and archives of many states, and to the Five Civilized Tribes Museum of Muskogee, for an unforgettable experience in dealing with highly specialized materials and situations, we also offer thanks.

To our personal teachers and trainers, still very much alive, Gene Weltfish of Fairleigh Dickinson University, and Forrest Clements of the United States Department of State, we give equal thanks for the doors they first opened for us.

To those tireless workers in the study of Indian life: Mable Morrow, the Reverend Father Peter John Powell, Dorothy Dunn, Anne Nolan Clarke, Elinor Gregg, William Zimmerman, and the late Oliver La Farge, we owe deep gratitude for setting an enduring example of work and hope, and of selfless service to others.

And although it is not, perhaps, the usual thing to do, we thank our editor-publisher, William Targ, and our Grandmother Spider, Nannine Joseph, for the diligence with which they have prodded us and the patience with which they have waited for results.

Finally, our deepest personal thanks go to Laura Katz King, of East Orange, New Jersey; Benjamin and Shirley Rachlin, of Miami Beach, Florida, and the late Richard and Sydney Marriott, of Oklahoma City, for all the things which only they and we can know.

Bibliography

By actual count, 853 titles were consulted in writing this book. In addition, periodicals, serial publications, newspapers, magazines both technical and popular, and many, many documents in many, many archives were examined, much of the material available on microfilm for the first time.

The publications of the Smithsonian Institution and Bureau of American Ethnology, both annual reports and bulletins, have been consulted so frequently and consistently that we have decided not to list them separately but only to say that they are the final field documents and the absolute authorities without which anthropologists cannot work. The same can be said for the publications of the American Anthropological Association, the American Association for the Advancement of Science, the Viking Fund Publications in Anthropology, the American Ethnological Society, and the reports of the many Commissioners of Indian Affairs and investigative bodies of all descriptions.

We have culled valiantly and, it would seem, ineffectually to cut the list of titles to the bone. We are not ignorant of the literature of our science; we ran out of space. So call this a selective bibliography, if you like, and please assume that we read the other books too.

AM and CKR

Abel, Annie Heloise, *The History of Events Resulting in Indian Consolidation West of the Mississippi River*. Annual Report, 1906, Washington, D.C., American Historical Association, Vol. I (1908), p. 241.

Adair, John, *The Navajo and Pueblo Silversmith*. Norman, University of Oklahoma Press, 1946.

Alford, Thomas Wildcat, *Civilization* (told to Florence Drake). Norman, University of Oklahoma Press, 1936.

Allen, J. A., *The American Bisons, Living and Extinct*. Lexington, Kentucky, Kentucky Geological Survey, n.d., pp. 39–40.

American Anthropological Association, *The American Anthropologist*.

Amsden, Charles Avery, *Navaho Weaving*. Albuquerque, University of New Mexico Press, 1949.

——— *Prehistoric Southwesterners From Basket Maker to Pueblo*. Los Angeles, Southwest Museum, 1949.

Anderson, Edgar, *Plants, Man, and Life*. Boston, Little, Brown, and Company, 1952.

Astrov, Margot, ed., *The Winged Serpent: An Anthology of American Indian Prose and Poetry*. New York, John Day, 1946.

Atkin, Edmond, *Indians of the Southern Colonial Frontier: Report and Plan of 1755* (ed. with intro. by Wilbur R. Jacobs). Columbia, University of South Carolina Press, 1954.

Bakeless, John, ed., *The Journals of Lewis and Clark*. New York, New American Library, 1964.

Bancroft, Herbert Howe, *The Native Races*. San Francisco, Bancroft, 1883.

Bandelier, Adolf, *The Delight Makers*. New York, Dodd, Mead and Company, 1947.

Bartram, William, *Travels in Georgia or Florida, 1773–74*. TransAmerican Philosophical Society, n.s., Vol. 33, p. 2.

Battey, Thomas C., *Life and Adventures of a Quaker Among the Indians* (ed. with intro. by Alice Marriott). Norman, University of Oklahoma Press, 1966.

Beard, Charles A., and Mary R., *The Beards' Basic History of the United States*. New York, Doubleday, 1960 (rev. ed.).

Betzinez, Jason, and Nye, Wilbur Sturtevant, *I Fought with Geronimo*. Harrisburg, Pennsylvania, The Stackpole Company.

Bienville, Jean Baptiste Le Moyne, *Sieur de Memoir: Mississippi Provincial Archives* (ed. by Rowland, Dunbar, and Sanders). Vol. III. Jackson, Mississippi, 1932.

Black, Glenn A., *Angel Site: An Archaeological, Historical, and Ethnological Study*. Indianapolis, Indiana Historical Society, 1967.

Bolton, Reginald Pelham, *Indian Remains in Northern Vermont*. Indian Notes Series, Vol. VII, No. 1. New York, Museum of the American Indian, Heye Foundation, 1930.

Bossu, N., *Travels Through That Part of North America Formerly Called Louisiana* (trans. by J. R. Forster). London, 1771.

Bourke, John G., *On the Border with Crook*. New York, Scribner's, 1891. Reprinted 1950 by Long's College Book Company, Columbus, Ohio.

Branch, E. Douglas, *The Hunting of the Buffalo*. Lincoln, University of Nebraska Press, 1962.

Broadhead, James O., *The Louisiana Purchase: Extent of Territory Acquired by Said Purchase*. St. Louis, Missouri Historical Society Publications, No. 13, 1897.

Bushnell, David I., Jr., "Various Uses of Buffalo Hair by the

North American Indians." *American Anthropologist*, n.s., Vol. II.

Canada Geographic Board, *Handbook of Indians of Canada.* Published as an appendix to the tenth report of the Geographic Board of Canada. Reprinted by permission of Mr. F. W. Hodge from *Handbook of American Indians North of Mexico,* published as Bulletin 30, Bureau of American Ethnology (ed. by F. W. Hodge). Ottawa, C. H. Parmelee, 1913.

Carroll, H. Bailey, and Haggard, J. Villasana, *Three New Mexico Chronicles.* Albuquerque, New Mexico, The Quivera Society, 1942.

Catlin, George, *Episodes from Life Among the Indians and Last Rambles* (ed. by Marvin C. Ross). Norman, University of Oklahoma Press, 1959.

——— *Letters and Notes on the Manners, Customs, and Condition of the North American Indians.* . . . 2 vols. London, published by the author, 1841.

Chouteau, Auguste, *Journal of the Founding of St. Louis.* Vol. III, No. 4. St. Louis, Missouri Historical Society, 1911.

The Chronicles of Oklahoma. Vol. XXIX, No. 2. Published quarterly by the Oklahoma Historical Society. Entire series.

Clark, W. P., *Indian Sign Language.* Philadelphia, Hamersly, 1885.

Clark, William, *The Field Notes of Captain William Clark, 1803–1805* (ed. by Ernest Staples Osgood). New Haven, Yale University Press, 1964.

Cohoe. A Cheyenne Sketchbook commentary by E. Adamson Hoebel and Karen Daniels Petersen. Norman, University of Oklahoma Press, 1964.

Cole, Cyrenus, *I Am a Man: The Indian Black Hawk.* Iowa City, Iowa, State Historical Society, 1938.

Cole, Fay Cooper, *et al., Kincaid: A Prehistoric Illinois Metropolis.* Chicago, University of Chicago Press, 1951.

Collier, Donald, *et al., Indians Before Columbus.* Chicago, University of Chicago Press, 1950.

Collier, John, *Indians of the Americas.* New York, Norton, 1947.

Cormack, Charles W., *et al., Papago Indian Pottery.* Seattle, University of Washington Press, 1962.

Crane, Leo, *Indians of the Enchanted Desert.* Boston, Little, Brown and Company, 1925.

Crook, General George, *Autobiography* (ed. and annotated by Martin F. Schmitt). Norman, University of Oklahoma Press, 1946.

Cross, Dorothy, *Archaeology of New Jersey.* Trenton, Archaeological Society of New Jersey, 1956.

——— *The Indians of New Jersey.* Trenton, Archaeological Society of New Jersey, 1953.

Cunninghame Graham, R. B., *The Horses of the Conquest*

(ed. by Robert Moorman Denhardt). Norman, University of Oklahoma Press, 1949.

Current Anthropology (A World Journal of the Science of Man). Sponsored by the Wenner-Gren Foundation for Anthropological Research, Inc. Vol. I, No. 1 (Jan., 1960), pp. 45–60.

Cushing, Frank Hamilton, *My Adventures in Zuni.* Santa Fe, New Mexico, Peripatetic Press, n.d.

Custer, Elizabeth B., *Following the Guidon.* Norman, University of Oklahoma Press, 1966 (new ed.).

Dale, Edward Everett, *The Indians of the Southwest.* Norman, University of Oklahoma Press, 1949.

Debo, Angie, *And Still the Waters Run.* Princeton, New Jersey, Princeton University Press, 1940.

Deuel, Thorne, "Basin Cultures of the Mississippi Valley." *American Anthropologist,* n.s., Vol. 37, No. 3, Pt. 1 (July–Sept., 1935).

Deuel, Thorne, ed., *Hopewellian Communities in Illinois.* Scientific Papers, Vol. V. Springfield, Illinois State Museum, 1952.

De Voto, Bernard, *The Year of Decision.* Boston, Little, Brown and Company, 1943.

Dockstader, Frederick J., *The Kachina and the White Man.* Bloomfield Hills, Michigan, Cranbrook Institute of Science, 1954.

Dorsey, George A., *The Cheyenne.* Part II, *The Sun Dance.* Chicago, 1905.

Douglas, Frederic Huntington, and d'Harnoncourt, René. *Indian Art of the United States.* New York, Museum of Modern Art, 1941.

Drucker, Philip, *Indians of the Northwest Coast.* Published for the American Museum of Natural History, Anthropological Handbook No. 10. New York, McGraw-Hill, 1955.

Duff, Wilson, *The Upper Stalo Indians: Anthropology in British Columbia.* Memoir No. 1, 1952.

Dutton, Bertha P., *Sun Father's Way.* Albuquerque, University of New Mexico Press, 1962.

Dyk, Walter, *Son of Old Man Hat.* New Haven, Yale University Press, 1939.

Eastman, Elaine Goodale, *Pratt, the Red Man's Moses.* Norman, University of Oklahoma Press, 1935.

Eggan, Fred, *Social Organization of the Western Pueblos.* Chicago, University of Chicago Press, 1950.

Emitt, Robert, *The Last War Trail: The Utes and the Settlement of Colorado.* Norman, University of Oklahoma Press, 1954.

Ewers, John C., *Indian Life on the Upper Missouri.* Norman, Oklahoma, University of Oklahoma Press, 1968.

——— *Plains Indians Painting: A Description of Aboriginal American Art.* Stanford, California, Stanford University Press, 1939.

Farb, Peter, *Man's Rise to Civilization as Shown by the Indians of North America, From Primeval Times to the Coming of the Industrial State*. New York, E. P. Dutton and Company, 1968.

Finney, Thomas M., *Pioneer Days With the Osage Indians, West of '96*. Bartlesville, Oklahoma, privately printed, 1925.

Forbes, Allan, *Some Indian Events of New England*. Boston, States Street Bank and Trust Company, 1934.

Ford, Clellan S., *Smoke From Their Fires: The Life of a Kuakiutl Chief*. New Haven, Yale University Press, 1941.

Foreman, Carolyn Thomas, *Indians Abroad, 1493–1938*. Norman, University of Oklahoma Press, 1943.

Foreman, Grant, *The Five Civilized Tribes*. Norman, University of Oklahoma Press, 1934.

——— *Indians and Pioneers: The Story of the American Southwest Before 1830*. Norman, University of Oklahoma Press, 1936 (rev. ed.).

——— *The Last Trek of the Indians*. Chicago, University of Chicago Press, 1946.

——— *Marcy and the Gold Seekers*. Norman, University of Oklahoma Press, 1939.

——— *Our Indian Ambassadors to Europe*. Missouri Historical Society Collections, Vol. V., No. 2. St. Louis, Missouri Historical Society, 1911.

Fowke, Gerard, *Surface Deposits Along the Mississippi Between the Missouri and the Ohio*. Missouri Historical Society Collections, Vol. III, No. 1. St. Louis, Missouri Historical Society, 1908.

Frost, Lawrence A., *The Court Martial of General George Armstrong Custer*. Norman, University of Oklahoma Press, 1969.

Fulton, Maurice Garland, ed., *Diary and Letters of Josiah Gregg*. Norman, University of Oklahoma Press, 1941.

Fundaburk, Emma Lila, and Foreman, Mary D., *Southeastern Indians: Life portraits*. A catalog of pictures, 1564–1860. Luverne, Alabama, Fundaburk, 1958.

——— *Sun Circles and Human Hands*. Luverne, Alabama, Fundaburk, 1957.

Gabriel, Ralph Henry, *Elias Boudinot: Cherokee and His America*. Norman, University of Oklahoma Press, 1941.

Garrard, Lewis H., *Wa-To-Yah*. Dodge City, Kansas, H. L. Carey, 1930.

Gibson, A. M., *The Kickapoos: Lords of the Middle Border*. Norman, University of Oklahoma Press, 1963.

Gillmor, Frances, *Traders to the Navajos*. Albuquerque, University of New Mexico Press, 1952.

Gladwin, Harold S., *Excavations at Snaketown*. Vol. II. Cambridge, Massachusetts, Peabody Museum, 1930.

——— *History of the Ancient Southwest*. Portland, Maine, Bond Wheelwright Company, 1957.

——— *Men Out of Asia.* New York, McGraw-Hill, 1947.

Goddard, Pliny Earle, *Indians of the Northwest Coast.* New York, American Museum of Natural History, 1934.

Goddard, Pliny Earle, *Indians of the Southwest.* New York, American Museum of Natural History, 1931.

Goldfrank, Esther S., ed., *The Artist of "Isleta Paintings" in Pueblo Society.* Washington, D.C., Smithsonian Press, 1967.

——— *Isleta Paintings.* Washington, D.C., Smithsonian Institution, 1962.

Grant, Campbell, *Rock Art of the American Indian.* New York, Thomas Y. Crowell, 1967.

Gregg, Elinor D., *The Indians and the Nurse.* Norman, University of Oklahoma Press, 1965.

Gregory, Jack, and Strickland, Rennard, *Sam Houston with the Cherokees, 1829–1833.* Austin, University of Texas Press, 1967.

Griffin, James B., *Handbook of American Archaeology.* Chicago, University of Chicago Press, 1952.

Grinnell, George Bird, *Cheyenne Indians.* 2 vols. New York, Cooper Square, 1962.

——— *Fighting Cheyennes.* Norman, University of Oklahoma Press, 1956.

Gunther, Erna, *Indians of the Northwest Coast.* Published by the Taylor Museum of the Colorado Springs Fine Arts Center and the Seattle Art Museum to accompany an exhibition of Northwest Indian art, 1951.

Hagan, William, *Sac and Fox Indians.* Norman, University of Oklahoma Press, 1958.

Haines, Francis, "Horses for Western Indians." *The American West,* Vol. III, No. 2 (Spring, 1966).

——— *The Nez Percés.* Norman, University of Oklahoma Press, 1955.

Hanks, Lucien M. J., and Richardson, Jane, *Tribe Undertrust: A Study of the Blackfoot Reserve in Alberta.* Toronto, Canada, University of Toronto Press, 1950.

Hawkes, E. W., and Linton, Ralph, *A Pre-Lenape Site in New Jersey.* Philadelphia, University of Pennsylvania Museum. (Published in *Anthropology,* Vol. VI, No. 3.)

Hawley, Florence, *Tree-ring Analysis and Dating in the Mississippi Drainage.* University of Chicago, Occasional Paper, No. 2, 1941.

Hoebel, E. Adamson, *The Cheyennes: Indians of the Great Plains.* New York, Holt, 1960.

Hofstadter, Richard *et al., The American Republic.* Vol. II. Englewood Cliffs, New Jersey, Prentice-Hall, 1959.

Hoig, Stan, *The Sand Creek Massacre.* Norman, University of Oklahoma Press, 1961.

Horgan, Paul, *Conquistadors in North American History.* Greenwich, Connecticut, Fawcett, 1963.

Hornaday, William T., *Extermination of the American Bison.* Annual report of the Board of Regents of the Smithsonian Institution, Pt. II, 1887, p. 373.

Hubbell, W. D., *The First Steamboats on the Missouri* (ed. by Vivian K. McLarty). Columbia, Missouri, State Historical Society of Missouri, 1957. (*Missouri Historical Review,* Vol. LI, No. 4.)

Huxley, Aldous, *The Doors of Perception.* New York, Harper and Brothers, 1954.

Hyde, George E., *Life of George Bent.* Norman, University of Oklahoma Press, 1968.

——— *A Sioux Chronicle.* Norman, University of Oklahoma Press, 1956.

Iliff, Flora Gregg, *People of the Blue Water.* New York, Harper and Brothers, 1954.

Jackson, Donald, ed., *Black Hawk: An Autobiography.* Urbana, University of Illinois Press, 1955.

——— *Letters of the Lewis and Clark Expedition: With Related Documents, 1783–1854.* Urbana, University of Illinois Press, 1962.

Jenness, Diamond, "The Faith of a Coass Salish Indian." *Anthropology in British Columbia,* Nos. 2–3 (1955).

Joffee, Natalie Frankel, *The Fox of Iowa.* New York, Appleton-Century, 1940. (Rep. from *Acculturation in Seven American Indian Tribes.*)

Jones, Douglas C., *The Treaty of Medicine Lodge.* Norman, University of Oklahoma Press, 1966.

Josephy, Alvin, *Our Indian Heritage.* New York, Knopf, 1968.

Kappler, Charles J., *Indian Affairs: Laws and Treaties.* Vol. II, *Treaties.* Washington, D.C., Government Printing Office, 1904.

Kelsey, F. E., *The Pharmacology of Peyote.* Vermillion, South Dakota, Department of Physiology and Pharmacology, State University of South Dakota, 1962.

Kent, Kate Peck, *Montezuma Castle Archaeology.* Southwest Monuments Association of Technical Series, Vol. III, No. 2. Denver, Colorado, Denver Art Museum, 1954.

Kenton, Edna, ed., "The Indians of North America." *The Jesuit Relations and Allied Documents. . . .* 2 Vols. New York, Harcourt, Brace, 1927.

Kidder, Alfred Vincent, *Pecos, New Mexico: Archaeological Notes.* Papers of the Robert S. Peabody Foundation for Archaeology, Vol. V. Andover, Massachusetts, Phillips Academy, 1958.

Kilpatrick, Jack Frederick and Anna Gritts, *Muskogean Charm Songs Among the Oklahoman Cherokees.* Washington, D.C., Smithsonian Press, 1967.

——— *The Shadow of Sequoyah.* Norman, University of Oklahoma Press, 1965.

Kluckhohn, Clyde, and Leighton, Dorothea, *The Navaho.* Cambridge, Harvard University Press, 1951.

Kneale, A. H., *Indian Agent*. Caldwell, Idaho, Caxton Printers, 1950.

Knight, Oliver, *Following the Indian Wars*. Norman, University of Oklahoma Press, 1960.

Kraenzel, Carl Frederick, *The Great Plains in Transition*. Norman, Oklahoma, University of Oklahoma Press, 1955.

Krause, Aurel, *The Tlingit Indians* (trans. by Erna Gunther). Seattle, University of Washington Press, 1956.

Kroeber, A. L., *Cultural and Natural Areas of Native North America*. Berkeley, University of California Press, 1953.

Kroeber, Theodora, *Ishi in Two Worlds*. Berkeley, University of California Press, 1961.

La Barre, Weston, *The Peyote Cult*. Yale University Publications in Anthropology, No. 19. New Haven, Yale University Press, 1938.

La Farge, Oliver, ed., *The Changing Indian*. Norman, Oklahoma, University of Oklahoma Press, 1942.

La Farge, Oliver, "The Present Condition of Southwest Anthropology." *Arizona Quarterly*, Vol. II, No. I (Spring, 1955).

Laubin, Reginald and Gladys, *The Indian Tipi: Its History, Construction, and Use*. Norman, Oklahoma, University of Oklahoma Press, 1957.

Laufe, Abe, ed., *An Army Doctor's Wife on the Frontier: Letters from Alaska and the Far West, 1874–1878*. Pittsburgh, Pennsylvania, University of Pittsburgh Press, 1962.

Leckie, William H., *The Buffalo Soldiers*. Norman, University of Oklahoma Press, 1967.

Lesser, Alexander, *The Pawnee Ghost Dance Hand Game, a Study of Cultural Change*. New York, Columbia University Press, 1933.

Library of Congress, Manuscripts Division, Journal of a council at St. Louis between the chiefs of the Great Osage, Auguste Chouteau, and French officers, August 16, 1787. Papeles procedentes, de la Isla de Cuba, Legajo 200.

Linderman, Frank Bird, *Out of the North: A Brief Historical Sketch of the Blackfeet Indian Tribe*. St. Paul, Minnesota, Great Northern Railway, 1947.

Lowie, Robert H., *The Crow Indians*. New York, Farrar and Rinehart, 1935.

——— *Indians of the Plains*. Published for the American Museum of Natural History. American Museum Science Books, 1963.

Lyford, Carrie A., *Ojibwa Craft (Chippewa)*. Department of Interior, Bureau of Indian Affairs, Washington, D.C., 1953.

McCallum, Henry D., and Frances T., *The Wire That Fenced the West*. Norman, University of Oklahoma Press, 1965.

MacGowan, Kenneth, and Hester, J. A., *Early Man in the New World*. Garden City, Doubleday and Company, 1962.

McGregor, John C., *Southwestern Archaeology*. New York, Wiley, 1941.

McGuire, Joseph D., *Pipes and Smoking Customs of the American Aborigines, Based on Material in the National Museum*. No imprint, no date. Probably Washington, D.C., Government Printing Office, 1899.

MacKay, Douglas, *The Honorable Company: A History of the Hudson's Bay Company*. Toronto, McClelland and Stewart, 1949 (rev. ed.).

McKenney, Thomas L., and Hall, James, *History of the Indian Tribes of North America*. Edinburgh, 1933.

MacNeesh, Richard S., *Summary of Archaeological Investigations in Southeastern Manitoba*. Canada Department of Northern Affairs and Natural Resources (from Bulletin No. 142, Annual Report of the National Museum for the Fiscal Year 1954–55).

McReynolds, Edwin C., *The Seminoles*. Norman, University of Oklahoma Press, 1957.

Marcy, Randolph B., *Adventure on Red River* (ed. by Grant Foreman). Norman, University of Oklahoma Press, 1937.

Marriott, Alice, "The Cross Timbers as a Cultural Barrier." *Texas Geographical Magazine*, Vol. VII, No. 1 (1943).

——— *Greener Fields*. New York, Dolphin, 1962. Chapter 8.

——— *Maria: The Potter of San Ildefonso*. Norman, Oklahoma, University of Oklahoma Press, 1948.

——— *Sequoyah: Leader of the Cherokees*. New York, Random House, 1956.

——— *The Ten Grandmothers*. Norman, University of Oklahoma Press, 1945.

——— Unpublished field notes on the Cheyenne, Hopi, Kiowa, and Tewa Indians.

——— Unpublished paper on Oto.

——— *Winter-Telling Stories*. New York, Crowell, 1947.

Marriott, Alice, and Rachlin, Carol, *American Indian Mythology*. New York, Crowell, 1968.

Martin, Paul S., *et al.*, *Indians Before Columbus*. Chicago, University of Chicago Press, 1947.

Mason, Otis Tufts, *Indian Basketry: Studies in a Textile Art Without Machinery*. 2 Vols. New York, Doubleday, 1904.

Mathews, J. J., *The Osages*. Norman, University of Oklahoma Press, 1962.

Mayer-Oakes, William J., *Prehistory of the Upper Ohio Valley*. Pittsburgh, Pennsylvania, Annals of Carnegie Museum, 1955.

Mayhall, Mildred P., *The Kiowas*. Norman, University of Oklahoma Press, 1962.

Mead, Margaret, *Anthropologist at Work: The Writings of Ruth Benedict*. Boston, Houghton Mifflin, 1959.

Mooney, James, *Aboriginal Population of America North of Mexico*. Smithsonian Miscellaneous Collection, Vol. 80, No. 7.

Moorhead, Max L., *The Apache Frontier*. Norman, University of Oklahoma Press, 1968.

Morgan, Lewis H., *League of the Ho-de-Wo-Saw-Nee or Iroquois*. New York, Dodd, Mead, 1922.

——— *The Indian Journals, 1859–62* (ed. by Leslie A. White). Ann Arbor, University of Michigan Press, 1959.

Morse, Jedidiah, *Report to the Secretary of War of the United States, on Indian Affairs, Comprising a Narrative of a Tour Performed in the Summer of 1820. . . .* New Haven, Connecticut, S. Converse, 1822.

Murray, Keith A., *The Modocs and Their War*. Norman, University of Oklahoma Press, 1959.

Nabokov, Peter, *Two Leggings: The Making of a Crow Warrior* (based on a field manuscript by William Wildschut). New York, Thomas Y. Crowell, 1967.

Nasatir, A. P., ed., *Before Lewis and Clark: Documents Illustrating the History of the Missouri, 1785–1804*. 2 vols. St. Louis, Missouri, St. Louis Historical Documents Foundation, 1952.

Native American Church of Oklahoma. Incorporation papers (Oct. 10, 1918).

Nevins, Allan, and Commager, Henry Steele, *Pocket History of the United States*. New York, Pocket Library, 1951.

Newcomb, Franc Johnson, *Navaho Neighbors*. Norman, University of Oklahoma Press, 1966.

Niles' Weekly Register (containing political, historical, scientific, astronomical, statistical, and biographical documents, essays, and facts . . .). Printed and published by the editor at the Franklin Press, Baltimore, Maryland (Sept., 1811).

Nye, Wilbur Sturtevant, *Bad Medicine and Good: Tales of the Kiowas*. Norman, University of Oklahoma Press, 1962.

——— *Carbine and Lance: The Story of Old Fort Sill*. Norman, University of Oklahoma Press, 1937.

——— *Plains Indian Raiders:* The Final Phases of Warfare From the *Arkansas to the Red River*. Norman, University of Oklahoma Press, 1968.

Oklahoma, Constitution of the State of Oklahoma. Adopted in convention, July 16, 1907. Ratified September 17, 1907. In force November 6, 1907. XXIII–Miscellaneous, No. 11.

Oklahoma Historical Society, Indian Archives Division, *Indian and Pioneer History*. Interview 5992, Vol. 4, pp. 163–64. Grant Foreman Collection. Oklahoma City, Oklahoma.

Opler, Morris Edward, *An Apache Life-way*. Chicago, University of Chicago Press, 1941.

Orchard, William C., *Sandals and Other Fabrics From Kentucky Caves*. New York, Museum of American Indians, 1920.

Parkman, Francis, *The Oregon Trail*. Garden City, New York, Doubleday, 1946 (also, Mentor, 1950).

Parsons, Elsie Clews, *Pueblo Indian Religion*. Chicago, University of Chicago Press, 1939.

Phillips, Paul Chrisler, *The Fur Trade*. 2 vols. Norman, University of Oklahoma Press, 1961.

Pike, Zebulon Montgomery, *The Southwestern Expedition of Zebulon M. Pike* (ed. by Milo Milton Quaife). Chicago, Lakeside Press, 1925.

Point, Nicolas, S. J., *Wilderness Kingdom: Indian Life in the Rocky Mountains, 1840–1847* (trans. with intro. by Joseph E. Donnelly). New York, Holt, Rinehart, Winston, 1967.

Powell, Reverend Father Peter John, Unpublished Cheyenne field notes.

Pratt, Richard Henry, *Battlefield and Classroom: Four Decades with the American Indian, 1867–1904* (ed. Robert M. Utley). New Haven, Yale University Press, 1964.

Qoyawayma, Polingaysi, and Vada, V. F. Carlson, *No Turning Back*. Albuquerque, University of New Mexico Press, 1964.

Rachlin, Carol K., *The Historic Position of Proto-Historic Cree Fabrics in the Textile Complex of Eastern North America*. Ottawa, National Museum of Canada, 1960.

——— *Historical Reconstruction From a Fossil Fabric, Angel Mounds Site, Newburgh, Indiana*. Bulletin, Indiana Historical Society, 1955.

——— *Native American Indian Church in Oklahoma*. Chronicles, Vol. XLII, No. 3, pp. 262–72.

——— Personal field notes, research among the Sauk Indians in Oklahoma, 1958–64.

——— *Sauk and Fox Weaving*. Unpublished manuscript on file with the American Museum of Natural History.

——— "Tight Shoe Night." *Mid Continent American Studies Journal*, Vol. 6, No. 2, pp. 84–100.

Radin, Paul, *The Autobiography of a Winnebago Indian*. New York, Dover, 1963.

Ray, Verne F., *Primitive Pragmatists: The Modoc Indians of North California*. Seattle, University of Washington Press, 1963.

Ritchie, William A., *The Archaeology of New York State*. Garden City, New York, Natural History Press, 1965.

Roberts, John M., *Zuni Daily Life*. Notebook No. 3. University of Nebraska, 1956.

Rouse, Irving, *A Survey of Indian River Archaeology, Florida*. New Haven, Yale University Press, Publications in Anthropology, No. 44, 1951.

Ruby, Robert H., and Brown, John, *Half-Sun on the Columbia: A Biography of Chief Moses*. Norman, University of Oklahoma Press, 1965.

Ruth, Kent, *Great Day in the West: Forts, Posts, and Rendezvous Beyond the Mississippi*. Norman, University of Oklahoma Press, 1963.

St. Louis Mercantile Library, Chouteau manuscripts. Nos. 14, 20, and 21.

Sandoz, Mari, *The Buffalo Hunters: The Story of the Hide Men*. New York, Hastings House, 1954.

——— *Cheyenne Autumn*. New York, McGraw-Hill, 1953.

Schroeder, Albert H., and Matson, Dan S., *A Colony on the Move: Gaspar Castaño de Sosa's Journal, 1590–1591*. School of American Research, 1965.

Schultes, Richard Evans, "Peyote (*Lophophora Williamsii*) and Plants Confused With It." Cambridge, Harvard University, Botanical Museum Leaflets, Vol. 5, No. 5, pp. 61–88, November 19, 1937.

Seger, John H., *Early Days Among the Cheyenne and Arapaho Indians* (ed. Stanley Vestal). Norman, University of Oklahoma Press, 1956.

Simmons, Leo W., ed., *Sun Chief: The Autobiography of a Hopi Indian*. Published for Institute of Human Relations. New Haven, Yale University Press, 1942.

Simpson, George Gaylord, *Horses*. Garden City, New York, Doubleday, 1961.

Skinner, Alanson, *Material Culture of the Menomini*. New York, Museum of the American Indian, Heye Foundation, 1921.

Slotkin, J. S., *The Peyote Religion*. Glencoe, Illinois, The Free Press, 1956, pp. 60–71.

Sonnichsen, C. L., *The Mescalero Apaches*. Norman, University of Oklahoma Press, 1958.

Speck, Frank G., *Naskapi: The Savage Hunters of the Labrador Peninsula*. Norman, University of Oklahoma Press, 1935.

Spier, Leslie, *Klamath Ethnography*. Berkeley, University of California Publications in American Archaeology and Ethnology, Vol. 30, 1930.

——— *Yuman Tribes of the Gila River*. Chicago, University of Chicago Press, 1933.

Stands-in-Timber, John, and Liberty, Margot, with Utley, Robert M., *Cheyenne Memories*. New Haven, Yale University Press, 1967.

Starkey, Marion L., *The Cherokee Nation*. New York, Alfred A. Knopf, 1946.

Steiner, Stan, *The New Indians*. New York, Harper & Row, 1968.

Stubbs, Stanley A., *Bird's-eye View of the Pueblos*. Norman, University of Oklahoma Press, 1950.

Tax, Sol (director), *Documentary History of the Fox Project, 1948–1959*. Chicago, University of Chicago Press, 1960.

"The Man They Ate for Dinner." *Time* (May, 1968), p. 98.

Thomas, A. B., *After Coronado*. Norman, University of Oklahoma Press, 1935.

Thwaites, Reuben Gold, ed., *Original Journals of the Lewis and Clark Expedition*. 8 vols. New York, Dodd, 1904.

Tibbles, Thomas Henry, *Buckskin and Blanket Days*. Garden City, New York, Doubleday, 1957.

Underhill, Ruth M., *First Penthouse Dwellers of America*. New York, Augustin, n.d.

——— *The Navahos*. Norman, University of Oklahoma Press, 1956.

——— *Red Man's America*. Chicago, University of Chicago Press, 1953.

United States Department of Agriculture, "Soils and Men." *Yearbook of Agriculture, 1938*. Washington, D.C., Government Printing Office, 1938.

United States Department of Labor, Bureau of the Census, Information given verbally to Carol K. Rachlin, 1962.

United States Department of the Interior, Office of Indian Affairs, *Indians at Work*. A newssheet for Indians and the Indian service. Washington, D.C., Government Printing Office, 1935.

United States Department of the Interior, *Final Report of the United States De Soto Expedition Commission*. Washington, D.C., Government Printing Office, 1939.

United States Department of the Interior, Bureau of Indian Affairs, *Report to the Secretary of the Interior by the Task Force on Indian Affairs*. Washington, D.C., Government Printing Office, 1961.

United States House of Representatives, 46th Congress, Second Session, *Testimony in Relation to the Ute Indian Outbreak Taken by the Committee on Indian Affairs of the House of Representatives, May 1, 1880*. Washington, D.C., Government Printing Office, 1880.

Vaillant, George C., *Aztecs of Mexico*. Suffolk, England, Penguin Books, 1956.

Villagrá, Gaspar Pérez de, *History of New Mexico* (trans. by Gilberto Espinosa). Los Angeles, The Quivera Society, 1933.

Wallace, Ernest, and Hoebel, E. Adamson, *The Comanches, Lords of the Southern Plains*. Norman, University of Oklahoma Press, 1952.

Wedel, Waldo R., *Prehistoric Man on the Great Plains*. Norman, University of Oklahoma Press, 1961.

Weltfish, Gene, *Lost Universe*. New York, Basic Books, 1965.

——— *Origins of Art*. Indianapolis, Indiana, Bobbs-Merrill, 1953.

Wheelwright, Mary C., *The Myths and Prayers of the Great Star Chant and the Myth of the Coyote Chant*. Santa Fe, New Mexico, Museum of Navajo Ceremonial Art, 1956.

White, E. E., *Experiences of a Special Indian Agent*. Norman, University of Oklahoma Press, 1965.

Wissler, Clark, *The American Indian*. New York, Douglas C. McMurtree, 1917.

Wormington, H. M., *Ancient Man in North America*. Denver Museum of Natural History, 1949.

——— *Prehistoric Indians of the Southwest*. Denver, Colorado Museum of Natural History, 1947.

Index